AMERICAN ASSOCIATION OF COLLEGIATE REGISTRARS AND ADMISSIONS OFFICERS

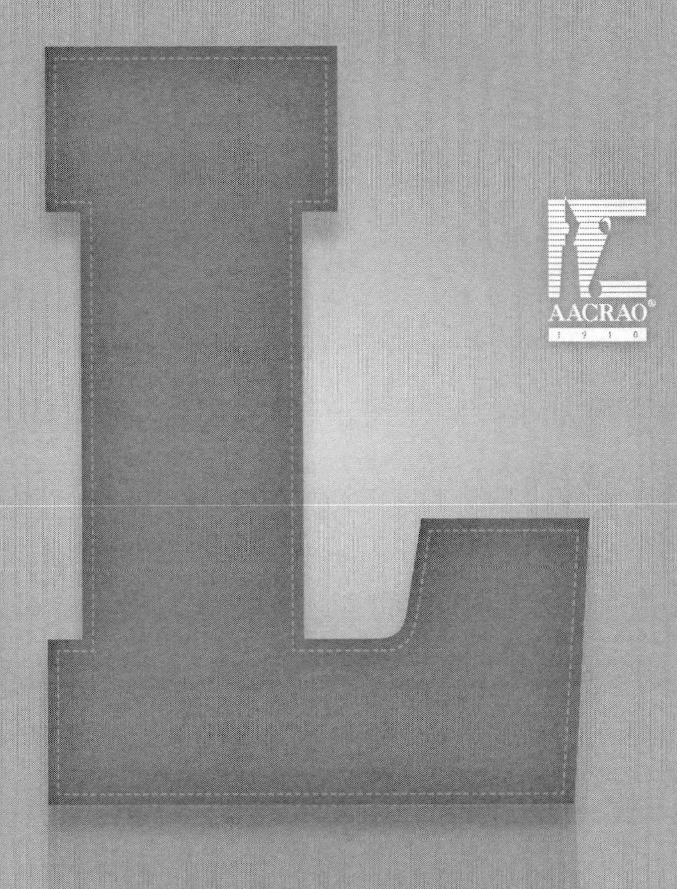

LEADERSHIP LESSONS

VISION AND VALUES FOR A NEW GENERATION

EDITED BY Louise Lonabocker & Heather Zimar

American Association of Collegiate
Registrars and Admissions Officers
One Dupont Circle, NW, Suite 520
Washington, DC 20036–1135

Tel: (202) 293–9161 | Fax: (202) 872–8857 | www.aacrao.org

For a complete listing of AACRAO publications, visit www.aacrao.org/publications/.

The American Association of Collegiate Registrars and Admissions Officers, founded in 1910, is a nonprofit, voluntary, professional association of more than 11,000 higher education administrators who represent more than 2,600 institutions and agencies in the United States and in forty countries around the world. The mission of the Association is to provide leadership in policy initiation, interpretation, and implementation in the global educational community. This is accomplished through the identification and promotion of standards and best practices in enrollment management, information technology, instructional management, and student services.

AACRAO adheres to the principles of non-discrimination without regard to age, color, handicap or disability, ethnic or national origin, race, religion, gender (including discrimination taking the form of sexual harassment), marital, parental or veteran status, or sexual orientation.

LIBRARY OF CONGRESS CATALOGING-IN-PUBLICATION DATA

Leadership lessons: vision and values for a new generation/edited by Louise Lonabocker; foreword by Jerry Sullivan.

pages cm

ISBN 978-1-57858-103-0

1. College registrars.
2. Educational leadership.
3. Student affairs services.
4. College personnel management.
5. Universities and colleges—Administration.

I. Lonabocker, Louise.

LB2341.L2683 2013
378.1'11—DC23
2012051368

Table of Contents

Dedicated to Jerry Sullivan, AACRAO Executive Director 1998–2012

Jerome (Jerry) Sullivan served as the Executive Director of AACRAO for fourteen years, from 1998 to 2012. His outstanding service to AACRAO and higher education resulted in a reinvigorated national organization. During those years, AACRAO priorities included sustainability and increased value for its members, including advocacy at the federal level. Jerry guided AACRAO through very lean years, and turned the financial position of the organization from critical lows to consistent strength. During Jerry's tenure, AACRAO focused on electronic standards, privacy issues in higher education, distance education, comparative international education research, and transfer credit.

Jerry's career in higher education began in 1966 at the University of Maine, and was followed by key administrative appointments at Kent State University, Iowa State University, and the University of Colorado at Boulder. Consistently known for innovation, he was among the early advocates of administrative process reengineering in higher education, and developed a national reputation for innovative uses of information technology to streamline service delivery on campuses where he worked. His contributions in this area resulted in a one-year appointment in 1995 to the U.S. Department of Education to lead the reengineering of the federal government's student financial aid delivery system. Jerry has written and lectured on a variety of topics ranging from process redesign to the student loan financing system. He holds a master's degree in public administration from the University of Maine.

Preface

For better or worse, I've spent 47 years in roles that demanded leadership for success. During that time I have read hundreds of books, articles, and essays on leadership. What they all have in common is a short list of leadership skills or behaviors; no single one, in my mind, particularly helpful in the long run. Hollywood, of course, usually gives the worst examples of leadership by presenting domineering generals or hard charging CEOs.

Those of us who are practitioners know that circumstances and changing times require a leader to constantly adapt and rebalance personal preferences against what is required for organizational success, and that no set of rigid principles will ever see us through. In particular, the public non-profit sector is led by shifting stakeholders who are not shy about demanding outcomes that favor their particular needs. Here, the ability to adapt to the situation is the only way to succeed.

I am pleased with the diversity of leadership styles described in *Leadership Lessons* and the underlying themes of adapting to new conditions to achieve organizational success. Leadership requires constant balancing, and I am honored to be associated with such a tremendous publication.

Jerry Sullivan
AACRAO Executive Director 1998–2012

Introduction

At the AACRAO Annual Meeting in Seattle in 2011, we were panelists in a session called Writing for AACRAO where some audience members pointed to a gap in the AACRAO literature about leadership. Several people agreed to write articles on the subject and Wayne Childs, now retired from Brigham Young University, offered to invite additional professionals to write short articles on leadership for *College and University*. The goal was to pass on stories to the next generation about how leaders came to be where they are, including their values, vision, and lessons learned.

As these articles arrived, we realized that we loved reading them and because Louise has been a devoted fan of Manager's Corner in the Sunday New York Times and the resulting book, she cast the net wider and invited other experienced professionals to contribute to a book about leadership. We're delighted that the seed planted in Seattle, nurtured by Wayne Childs, resulted in articles with themes that we never would have envisioned. The writers share many common core values and give voice to similar practices, but they have independently shaped their articles in ways that inspire, motivate, and may even bring a tear to your eye.

Since the leadership series originated with Wayne Childs, we begin with his article in which he writes about becoming an educational leader, and more specifically an educator, reminding us that we will become better leaders by teaching others what we know. He speaks to the value of self-awareness, problem solving, advocacy, and bridge building.

Dan Bender advises newcomers and established members of the profession to think about their role in the profession, and to think about themselves as professionals. Dan reminds us that being a professional implies a commitment to the profession, involvement in setting standards and practices, lifelong learning, and ethical behavior.

Meredith Braz draws on the theme of the registrar as an inconspicuous leader, often unseen and sometimes unsung, yet quite present and surprisingly influential. She succeeds by developing trust, planning strategically, and taking action to achieve outcomes, which at the end of the day is all that matters.

Sharon Cramer draws on her experience as the leader of a student system implementation to encourage enrollment professionals to look at exceptional circumstances in a new way, as a greenhouse for facilitating the development of leadership perspectives and unique opportunities for mentoring. She reminds us that these painful times can offer chances for learning and growth.

Hansford Epes, a 35-year professor of German turned registrar, knew he would have to learn and lead, instantly. He describes his felicitous transition to a profession of procedures, politics and people, and explains how the act of learning is itself an act of leadership.

Susan Gottheil traces her career starting with her days as a student activist before she, like many of us, found herself working as a student employee in a campus office. Realizing that change could come from within, she documents a career where she led change, took risks, and strove to make a difference in the lives of others.

Karen Gualtieri shares management epiphanies including ways to lead by example, pinpoint talent, learn from decisions gone wrong, and understand what it takes to accomplish the work.

Bill Haid has adopted a leadership style that he refers to as leadership by respect. He defines his style with a set of core values, explains how he puts these into practice in the workplace, and concludes with examples from his AACRAO and campus experiences.

Christine Kerlin grounds her reflections on leadership in the theory of Warren Bennis and John W. Gardner and writes about building a shared vision and the contagion that spreads from an overriding passion for the promise of what we are doing.

Gary Kramer explains how the bellwether, originally the sheep who led the flock, now refers to a leader or pacesetter. He shows how today's bellwethers can lead, promote their own success, and promote student success by fostering the five C's of bellwethers.

Susan Leigh came to her enrollment management leadership role after a 20-year career in theatre. She draws on her experience as an actor and director to create a vision of the future that propels people toward it. She reminds us that we all bring unique skills and interests, and encourages us to draw on those to fuel our contributions.

Paul Marthers spent his formative years in a cheese factory where he was tapped at the tender age of 16 to lead the block cheddar crew. Now a vice president, he offers leadership lessons learned from a career that has taken him from the east coast to the west coast and back, working at nine different institutions.

Bryan Newton's passion for higher education is evident in his expressed gratitude for a career as a higher education leader and scholar. He encourages young leaders to strive for excellence, learn from failure, help develop followers, and exercise flexibility by gaining an understanding of each individual's situation.

Lisa Mosele Scully tells about the importance of leading from the heart, building an office culture of mutual respect and trust, and fostering open communication.

Clayton Smith draws on the wisdom of Dumbledore of Harry Potter fame and proves that mentors are everywhere, within and outside the profession. He encourages us to seek them out, ask for help, and stay connected. He also reminds us of our duty to the next generation.

Paul and Kim Taylor first met twelve years ago at a state conference. So, it comes as no surprise that they share a passion for the leadership opportunities resulting from involvement in state, regional, and national professional associations. See how they walk the talk when it comes to volunteering, mentoring, and networking.

Roger Thompson quotes Yogi Berra and recommends a leadership style personified by decisive action. He notes the importance of empowering others to make decisions close to the source, and explains how he once rewarded and energized staff by taking them on a cruise!

Sue Van Voorhis began to think more seriously about leadership six years ago when she realized over half the staff in her division were eligible to retire soon. She writes about a career grounded in listening, a lesson learned as a young child running for school "president for a day."

Jim Wager begins with a leadership lesson learned from his grandfather before describing five key leadership traits including discipline, humility, accountability, perseverance, and vision.

Janet Ward challenges us to consider how we want to be remembered and offers lessons learned over a career that exposed her to the range of functions within enrollment services. Her humanistic philosophy is supplemented with practical advice and creative solutions.

Beth Weckmueller is in the midst of a career transition, moving to a new role where she will focus on planning and policy development. She took the opportunity to reflect on the mentoring of younger colleagues, and encourages aspiring professionals to find their own style, characterized by authenticity, equanimity, compassion, and humility.

We conclude with an article Louise wrote reflecting on her 40-year career at Boston College. She writes about hiring and retaining outstanding staff, embracing change, and the importance of communication and data-based decision making. She reminds us that relaxation and balance often impacts our professional insight.

We would like to thank Kelly Stern for her assistance with copy editing. We hope you will enjoy these articles as much as we have and will share this book with colleagues who can benefit from the lessons learned by these remarkable, wise, and wonderful professionals who represent a collective total of roughly 500 years in the business.

Louise Lonabocker
Director of Student Services and University Registrar,
Boston College
Editor-in-Chief, *College and University*

Heather Zimar
Managing Editor, *SEM Quarterly; College and University*

About the Authors

Daniel J. Bender

Daniel Bender is Assistant Dean for Academic Affairs and Registrar at the University of the Pacific, Arthur A. Dugoni School of Dentistry in San Francisco, CA. In 2005 he earned an Ed.D. in Learning and Instruction from the University of San Francisco. He is an active member of AACRAO and the American Dental Education Association, and has been an officer, presenter, and facilitator at national meetings for both groups. Dr. Bender's research interests include race and gender issues in health care and health care education, diversity and inclusion, student support services, teaching and learning, and faculty development.

Meredith Braz

Meredith Braz is a graduate of St. Lawrence University in Canton, N.Y., and she received a Master of Arts in Teaching from Smith College. She spent fifteen years in the Bates College registrar's office, starting as Assistant Registrar in 1991 and progressing to Registrar and Administrative Dean for Academic Systems before coming to Dartmouth as Registrar of the College. Prior to her tenure at Bates, she taught in Massachusetts and Vermont schools. Braz also worked in the Sophia Smith Collection, a Women's History Archive at Smith College, at Williston-Northampton School and at the Yarmouth Historical Society. She has done consulting work for the American University of Kuwait.

Braz has served as Vice President for Professional Development and as President of the New England Association of Collegiate Registrars and Admissions Counselors (NEACRAO). She has also served as a member of the AACRAO task force to study the impact of utilizing outsourcing in Registrar and Admissions offices, as a member of the AACRAO Public Policy Committee, and as a member of the Nominations and Elections Committee.

M. Wayne Childs

Wayne Childs has worked in academic student services at Brigham Young University (BYU) for the past 30 years. He has served as Associate Registrar and Director of Assessment and Planning. He earned his master's and education specialist degrees in Education Leadership and his doctorate in Higher Education Leadership from BYU.

Sharon F. Cramer

Sharon Cramer, Ph.D. is a SUNY Distinguished Service Professor Emerita. During her career at Buffalo State College, (1985–2011), she served in many roles, including faculty member, Department Chair, and Chair of the College Senate. From 1999 to 2004, she was Executive Director of the SABRE Project, an implementation of the Oracle Student System for web-based delivery of student services. She was an officer, on the Board of Directors, of four professional and governance organizations, and received the highest award from each of them during her career.

Her publications include *Student Information System: A Guide to Implementation Success* (2005) as well as articles in *College and Uni-*

versity (2003). Dr. Cramer has given over 100 presentations and keynotes in 20 states and Canada. She completed her Ph.D. studies at New York University, earned an M.A.T. from Harvard University and a B.A. from Tufts University. She has been listed in Who's Who in America and Who's Who in American Education since 2006.

Hansford M. Epes

Hansford Epes is Registrar Emeritus and Professor Emeritus of German and Humanities at Davidson College. Originally from Lynchburg, Virginia, Hansford obtained a Bachelor of Arts in English and German from Davidson College and a Ph.D. from the University of North Carolina in Germanic Languages and Literatures. He served as Professor of German and Humanities at Davidson College from 1964 to 2012, and was recognized with the Sears-Roebuck Foundation Award for Teaching Excellence and Campus Leadership, the Omicron Delta Kappa award for Leadership and the Thomas Jefferson Award. A teacher at heart, Hansford continued teaching while serving as the Registrar for Davidson College from 2000 to 2012.

He is a member of SACRAO and AACRAO, and served on the Editorial Advisory Board for *College and University* from 2001 to 2012. Epes' career has not been all work and no play; he has acted, directed, coached College Bowl teams and even appeared on Jeopardy four times in 1993!

Susan Gottheil

Susan Gottheil has more than 30 years of leadership experience in the Canadian postsecondary sector helping institutions to promote and expand academic programs, increase student recruitment and retention, enhance learning and development, improve student and academic support services, and promote collaborative partnerships. With an undergraduate degree from McGill University and an M.A. in Women's History, Susan began her career at Vanier College CEGEP in Montreal where she spent nine years teaching before moving into senior administrative positions at Carleton University. In 2006, she moved to western Canada to help Mount Royal transition from a college to a university and roll out new undergraduate degree programs. Susan currently serves as Vice-Provost (Students) at the University of Manitoba, and has also helped a number of Canadian institutions develop strategic enrolment plans in her role as Senior Consultant with AACRAO Consulting. Susan and Clayton Smith have organized the Canadian SEM Summit over the past five years and co-edited the 2011 AACRAO book *SEM In Canada: Promoting Student and Institutional Success in Canadian Colleges and Universities.*

Karen P. Gualtieri

Karen Gualtieri has served at Rockland Community College, a unit of the State University of New York, as Registrar, Dean of Enrollment Management, and Vice President of Student Development. Previously she worked at Orange County Community College as Assistant to the Dean for Academic Services and as a Management Analyst/Health Care Planner with the Veterans Administration. She received her Bachelor of Arts summa cum laude and her Master's of Public Administration from Ohio State University.

William R. Haid

William Haid is University Registrar at the University of California–San Diego. He previously served as Assistant Vice President for Enrollment and Access and Executive Director of Enrollment Services at Colorado State University. In his career, Bill has always placed an emphasis on organizational development for his teams and career development for those with whom he has worked. Of all the experiences, accomplishments, and achievements from a career as registrar and enrollment manager at large public institutions, what Bill cherishes most is the growth, development, and advancement of so many of the people he has mentored over the years, who have also risen to positions of leadership in their professional careers. Bill is an AACRAO Past President (1999–2000) and has served in leadership roles in AACRAO, RMACRAO and NMACRAO. He has a bachelor's degree in Business Administration from San Jose State University and a Master of Business Administration from Arizona State University.

Christine Kerlin, Ed.D.

Christine Kerlin retired from the position of Vice President at Everett Community College, WA, having served in leadership roles for the University Center, Strategic Planning and Enrollment Management from 1996 to 2012. Prior to arriving at Everett in 1996, Christine served as Director of Admissions and Records at Central Oregon Community College and as the Director of Admissions at The Evergreen State College. She is currently a senior consultant for AACRAO Consulting.

Gary L. Kramer

Gary Kramer is Professor of Counseling Psychology and Special Education and Associate Director in the Center for the Improvement of Teacher Education Department, McKay School of Education, Brigham Young University. A former Dean of Students, Director of Student Services, and Associate Dean of Student Academic Services, Kramer received his Ph.D. from Oregon State University.

Susan Leigh

Susan Leigh joined DePaul University as faculty at the Theatre School, but is now Associate Vice President for Enrollment Management and Marketing. Susan oversees Student Records and led the creation of the DePaul Central offices, a one-stop for integrated student services that includes a contact center offering students answers to questions about student records, financial aid and student accounts. Susan did her undergraduate study in theatre at Rhode Island College in Providence, and earned her MFA in Acting from Temple University in Philadelphia. In addition, Susan was certified to teach speech for the stage by the late Edith Skinner. Her resume credits more than 100 productions nationally in both professional and university theatre. Most recently, Susan has taught as an Associate Professor in the Women and Gender Studies Department at DePaul, as well as the Study Abroad London Program, with a focus on the representation of gender onstage.

Louise Lonabocker

Louise Lonabocker is Executive Director, Student Services, and University Registrar at Boston College. She is a past president of AACRAO and editor-in-chief of *College and University.*

Paul P. Marthers, Ed.D.

Paul Marthers is Vice President for Enrollment at Rensselaer Polytechnic Institute (NY). Marthers has also worked at Reed College (OR), Oberlin College (OH), Phillips Academy (MA), Boston College (MA), Duke University (NC), Vassar College (NY), and Bennington College (VT). His articles have appeared in *Academe, American Educational History Journal, College and University, History of Education Quarterly, The Journal of College Admission, The Journal of Higher Education Outreach and Engagement, The Journal of Graduate Liberal Studies,* InsideHigherEd.com, Liberal Arts Online, *The School Counselor, University Business* and a chapter in *College Unranked* (published in 2005 by Harvard University Press). He is the author of *Eighth Sister No More: The Origins and Evolution of Con-*

necticut College (Peter Lang Publishing, 2011). A first generation college graduate, Marthers has a B.A. (English) from Oberlin College, a M.Ed. (counseling) from Boston University, a M.A. (liberal studies) from Reed College, and an Ed.D. (higher education management) from the University of Pennsylvania.

Bryan Newton

Bryan Newton is Associate Vice President of Marketing and Enrollment Management at Aiken Technical College in Aiken, SC. He has a B.A. from Southern Illinois University at Edwardsville and a J.D. from The Ohio State University College of Law. He is currently pursuing a Ph.D. in higher education leadership from Colorado State University.

Lisa Mosele Scully

Lisa Mosele Scully is Senior Assistant Registrar and Manager of Student Academic Records in the Office of the Registrar at Indiana University, Bloomington. She is a graduate of Indiana University Bloomington with a master's degree in College Student Personnel Administration and holds a Bachelor of Arts degree, with a major in English literature.

Clayton Smith

Clayton Smith is Vice-Provost, Students and International at the University of Windsor, where he also serves as Dean of Students. Smith has served as the University's Registrar and Secretary of Senate. Prior to becoming Vice-Provost, he held senior enrollment management positions at the State University of New York College of Agriculture and Technology at Cobleskill, Tallahassee Community College in Florida and the University of Maine at Augusta. Dr. Smith holds a Bachelor of Arts degree in Political Science from the University of Southern Maine, a Master of Arts degree in Political

Science from Drew University, a Master of Public Administration degree from the University of Maine, and a Doctor of Education degree in Higher Education from Florida State University. He currently serves on the editorial boards for *College and University*, *Journal of Student Affairs Research & Practice*, and the *Journal of International Students*, and he co-chairs the annual Canadian Strategic Enrollment Management Summit. Dr. Smith is a senior consultant with AACRAO Consulting and a frequent national and international presenter on strategic enrollment management, student engagement, student affairs and internationalization topics and has consulted at a wide range of postsecondary educational institutions in Canada, the U.S., and abroad.

Kim Taylor

Kim Taylor has spent 30 years in higher education as Registrar at Texas A & M Commerce, Registrar and Associate Director for Information Technology at Northern Kentucky, and as Associate Registrar at the University of Texas at Austin. She served on Texas ACRAO's N&E and Program Committee, as president of Kentucky ACRAO, as SACRAO Local Arrangements Chair, and is currently a Member at Large of SACRAO's Executive Committee.

Paul Taylor

Paul Taylor spent more than 30 years in higher education at the University of Kentucky and Lexington Community College, where he served as Dean and Vice President of Enrollment Management and Student Affairs. He has served as President of Kentucky ACRAO, SACRAO, and AACRAO. He has worked as a Regional Director at the National Student Clearinghouse since September 2005.

Roger J. Thompson

Dr. Roger Thompson is the Vice President for Enrollment Management, serving as the chief enrollment management officer for the University of Oregon, and is responsible for student recruitment and retention. During his tenure, enrollment at the University of Oregon has reached record levels for total enrollment, academic quality and diversity, both in terms of ethnicity and social economic status and international status. Additionally, freshmen-to-sophomore retention has increased to 86 percent, which is also a university record. Roger has been a frequent presenter at national and regional conferences throughout the country and has published in the areas of college choice, student persistence, student success, and affordability issues in higher education.

A native Oregonian, Roger served in similar positions at Indiana University and the University of Alabama prior to joining the University of Oregon. He earned a B.A. in Broadcasting from California State University, Long Beach; an M.S. from the University of Central Missouri; and a doctorate in Higher Education Policy and Administration from the University of Southern California.

Susan Van Voorhis

Sue Van Voorhis is Director of Academic Support Resources and University Registrar at the University of Minnesota. During her 25 years in this profession, she has led the successful implementation and enhancement of ERP software, the One Stop Student Services Center and the Office of Classroom Management for the University of Minnesota and previously at Montana State University, Bozeman. Van Voorhis, who has many other administrative assignments at the university, also was involved in the institution's conversion to semesters, renovation of several campus buildings, reengineering of university wide processes and policies, and also serves as a consultant to other colleges and universities. She regularly volunteers and presents at AACRAO and UMACRAO.

J. James Wager

James Wager is Vice-President and Chief Information Officer of SCRIP-SAFE® International, Inc. Before retiring from Pennsylvania State University after more than three decades of service, Wager served as Assistant Vice President for Enrollment Management and as University Registrar.

Janet Ward

Janet Ward has worked in higher education administration for 35 years. Since 1988 she has worked at Seattle Pacific University, beginning as University Registrar and today serving as Associate Vice President for Information and Data Management. Janet has also provided leadership within various higher education professional associations, including WACCRAO, PACRAO, and AACRAO. She is a graduate of Washington State University, and holds an MPA from The Evergreen State College.

Beth L. Weckmueller

Beth Weckmueller has had a long and distinguished career in higher education, primarily at the University of Wisconsin-Milwaukee where she has taught and held a variety of administrative positions related to admissions, records, registration and enrollment management. After serving for 15 years as the Executive Director of Enrollment Services, Weckmueller currently holds the position of Senior Associate for Enrollment Initiatives within the newly created Office of Enrollment Management at UW–Milwaukee. Among other publications, she is the co-editor (with M. Therese Ruzicka) of *Student Records Management: A Handbook* (The Greenwood Educators' Reference Collection, 1997).

I

CHAPTER ONE

Developing Leadership in Student Services

M. WAYNE CHILDS

I confess:

As a boy, I never once played "Registrar." I grew up on a farm where I neither saw nor ever heard the word. I remember seeing it for the first time above a doorway in the hall of the building that housed the administrative offices of the small, rural junior college I attended. I was sure the word had something to do with registration, but I was confident that it had been misspelled (seemed it had too many "r"s.) After graduating and transferring to a university, I came across the word again—spelled the same way—in the hallway of the administration building. Even though I still didn't know what the word meant, I started to get the idea that perhaps I was wrong about the spelling.

Now, having spent 38 years in education, I have a much better understanding of the duties and responsibilities of a university registrar. For most of my career, I served as a registrar at Brigham Young University (and yes, I learned how to spell the word). But most important, I have come to understand something—if only the tiniest bit—about leadership and what it requires to really make a difference in the lives of students as they pursue their education and life dreams. I hope that the lessons I share will be beneficial to all my colleagues, seasoned leaders as well as those new to the profession.

ON BECOMING AN EDUCATION LEADER

It takes a conscious effort to become an education leader. Usually, it doesn't "just happen." Start by making sure that you know what business you are in. Regardless of your academic background or your job description in student services, you should know with certainty that you are in the business of education. Even though your job may not be in a classroom, you are an educator by virtue of the fact that you work in education. This distinction is an important part of being a leader in student services because *leaders have clarity when it comes to their purpose and their mission.*

If you believe that your only purpose is to admit students, schedule classes, register students, and keep records, then you may not be correct. Ted Levitt, of the Harvard Business School, told his students, "People don't want a quarter-inch drill; they want a quarter-inch hole." His argument was that most people will focus on their product or the process and will neglect the benefit customers truly seek.

Railroads in the 1950s and 1960s made this same mistake: Decade after decade, they built bigger and better railroads because that was the business they thought they were in. But in reality, they were in the transportation business. Having lost sight of that fact, the railroads were nearly put out of business by airplanes. When students are trying to be admitted, trying to register, or trying to get their transcripts, remember that what they really want is not merely to be admitted, to register for courses, or to get their transcripts; the real reason they are at your institution is to further their education. *Becoming an educated person is the larger benefit that students seek.*

In the simplest terms, there are only two "elements" at colleges and universities: faculty and students. And these two elements exist for two purposes: teaching and learning. Everything else in higher education—including student services—is intended to support and facilitate the teaching and learning processes.

If you are clear that your true purpose is to be a part of the education process and not just to build bigger and better processes and systems, then you will be oriented in a way that will foster success in your work and in your career because you will be effective in your efforts to help students and faculty achieve the outcome of education.

LEADERSHIP STARTS WITH SELF

You don't need a title to be a leader. You don't need a big office, and you certainly don't need to have people report to you. *You become a leader by virtue of who you are.* That includes your core values and beliefs, how you think, how you behave and how you act, how you communicate your ideas, and, most important, how you treat people. What we need in the academy are *education leaders.* What we don't need are more education managers. The difference is substantial. One can manage time and money, but one cannot really manage people. People are creative, free-thinking individuals who want as much agency as possible to choose what they do. *Exercise your leadership by giving people choices whenever and wherever possible and by helping them make good decisions.*

Managers focus on the best way to get things done and so tend to control, dictate, and mandate procedures; leaders focus on the things they think are most important and then trust others to make good choices. Leaders stay focused on doing what they believe is right, and they teach those principles to others. *To become a leader, focus your time, your talents, and your energy on doing what you believe to be the right thing.*

Here are my ten best suggestions for becoming a leader by starting with self:

- Resist the need to always feel and be in control.
- Be a teacher of correct principles.

- Always treat others with kindness, even when you must say no and when you cannot give them what they want.
- Learn to understand that doing what is right is not always logical or objective; that is why it is often met with resistance.
- Focus on ideas rather than functions or processes.
- Be clear about your core values and what you believe. Your core values and beliefs should drive your actions. Leaders make decisions that are based on correct principles, not solely on rules, policy, or the expectations of others.
- Have a clear vision of the possibilities for your organization—possibilities that are based on its purpose.
- Empower others by showing trust when giving assignments.
- Surround yourself and build relationships with the best people you can find.
- Demonstrate confidence in the people you serve.

BE A PROBLEM SOLVER

Learn to be a problem solver. It is said that "necessity is the mother of invention." Start with small problems or circumstances that constitute a "necessity" and that are well within your control or stewardship. Consider what you can do that would make things easier, faster, or better for others. A problem solver is a person who makes things happen and who gets things done.

The following ideas and principles have been particularly helpful as I have worked to solve problems:

- As you seek to resolve problems, recognize that they may have more than one solution. Don't stop looking for solutions just because you find one that seems effective. Keep looking for the second, third, or fourth right answers.
- Changing behavior is not always the best solution. Trying harder, changing attitudes, being more diligent, or redoubling effort may not yield desired results. The solution may lie in trying

something different. In other words, *what* you do is more important than how "*hard*" you do it.

- Problems will persist if you rely ONLY on your strengths to identify solutions. Often, our strengths become weaknesses because we rely too heavily on them, habitually doing what we do best rather than seeking the best things to do. When your only tool is a hammer, you approach every problem as if it were a nail. Collaborate with others to identify solutions to problems.
- Learn to ask questions; learn to ask the right questions. "Problems" are circumstances with questions. Answers do not exist without questions.
- Problems can be difficult to solve because they often are misidentified. Fail to diagnose a problem correctly and you may end up with a good solution...to the wrong problem.
- Problems remain when we fail to act on our decisions and choose instead to keep talking.
- Take action, even if you don't think you are ready. Excuses and reasons for delay invariably are motivated by fear. Acknowledge fear, but take action. Fear and uneasiness are normal and possibly even healthy. Fear becomes a problem if you fail to confront it and so let it paralyze you.
- All solutions to problems require communication with feedback.
- "The problems that exist today cannot be solved with the same thinking that created them" (Albert Einstein).

BE AN ADVOCATE FOR STUDENTS

Hanging on the wall of the school where I first taught was a statement that read, "Nothing is more unequal than the equal treatment of unequals." I remind myself often that people are not all the same. Policies and procedures usually are written to address the needs of the institution—needs centered on order and conformity. No matter how unequal everyone is, policy and procedure are intended to ensure that everyone is treated equally. Education leaders advocate for students by balancing their needs with those of the institution. When a student can justify his action, help him by making an exception without harming or eroding institutional policy. Justifiable reasons may include circumstances beyond the student's control. Look for justifiable reasons to help students; don't expend all your energy defending and upholding policy.

Advocate for students by giving serious consideration to their appeals. Don't deny or approve students' requests in isolation, but collaborate with other stakeholders to identify justifiable reasons for approving (or denying) students' requests. Having spent years hearing student appeals, I have developed twelve questions that have guided others and myself in the decision-making process.

- Would the exception harm the university if it were approved?
- Would it be compassionate to approve the student's request?
- Will approving the request aid the student's quest for knowledge and perfection?
- Would it build goodwill and better friendship?
- Would it be fair to all concerned?
- Would approving the request be immoral or illegal?
- Is the problem a pattern of behavior for the student?
- How will this decision affect other stakeholders?
- Does the consequence fit the crime?
- What is the probability of this recurring and requiring further exceptions?
- Would it be expedient to approve the request?
- To what degree is the university culpable in the problem?

BE A BRIDGE BUILDER

Throughout my career, I have sought most to be considered a partner in the education process by students and faculty alike. Achieving this goal has required a proactive rather than a merely reactive approach to service. In other words, don't just sit in the metaphorical fire station waiting for the alarm: Get out there and prevent fires. There are many ways to build bridges and to make strong connections across the campus community. Start by involving all staff in your office in considering how this could be accomplished. Work with your cohorts to identify stakeholders and to discover how you could improve the lives of others—especially students. Volunteer for committees and other assignments and so demonstrate your willingness and commitment to help in any way possible. Do your work in ways that demonstrate that you and your office are team players. Above all, be a problem solver. Experience has taught that every time you help others on campus solve a problem, the "bridge" will get stronger.

FINAL CONFESSION AND CONCLUSION

I confess that most of the lessons I have learned over the years have been the result of someone who has been willing to teach me. In return, I have tried to teach others. Leaders are teachers, and we become better leaders by teaching others what we ourselves have learned. *Docendo discitur:* "one learns by teaching."

Decide to be a leader. Take time to clarify your purpose and your mission. Determine how you and those with whom you work can be more proactive and less reactive. Become a problem solver by identifying problems that can be fixed with a quick and effective solution. Advocate for students by making exceptions when they are needed and when there are justifiable reasons for so doing. And finally, strengthen relationships across campus. You will never have reason to regret it.

2

CHAPTER TWO

Reflections of a Professional School Registrar

DANIEL J. BENDER, ED.D.

It's an honor

to be invited to submit a reflective essay on lessons I have learned in my career. I flatter myself to think that if "pearls of wisdom" such as those presented here and in other essays in this series had been available to me 20 years ago, I might have had an easier path. In reality, I am not certain it would have helped. I had no idea where I would land when in my mid-30s I left a successful post-secondary classroom teaching practice for full-time administration. My initial exposure to the functions and importance of the registrar was in my first full-time administrative position, where I supervised a staff of ten, one of whom worked with the registrar's office to ensure our remote degree completion courses were recorded appropriately to the student's transcript. I wager that almost every registrar's story is unique, whether it began as a part-time work-study job in the registrar's office, or you stumbled into it by chance, learned to love it, and stayed (as in my case).

Regardless of the personal story, I believe there are skill sets that are critical to becoming and remaining a successful, effective registrar. The skill sets I present here are derived less from the management or education literature and more from personal experience. I did not do everything I recommend, and in retrospect I wish I had done more. The list is not exhaustive, but I suspect the reader will discover overlap between my reflections and those of other contributors—in and of itself a valuable lesson for the emerging registrar.

Beyond merely adding to a list of recommended behaviors, however, I would like to challenge the reader, be they an established or up-and-coming registrar, to begin thinking about our work and role in the educational enterprise as a *profession* and of yourself as a *professional.* By this I do not mean pay grade, what you wear to work, how large a staff you supervise, or whether you have preferred parking on campus. Being a *professional* implies having specialized and sometimes highly technical knowledge or training and using it to provide service and benefit to others. The relationship between a *professional* and the consumer of professional services is based on trust, because the consumer does not have the expertise, time, or interest in performing the work. A further hallmark of a *profession* is autonomy. *Professionals* are largely self-governing and self-policing; they agree as a group on how to define and perform their work and set the standards to which members of the profession adhere. Being a *professional* implies a commitment to the profession as a whole, to its growth and development as such, to lifelong learning and ethical behavior of its members, and to helping shape the next generation. Dentists, lawyers, physicians, and architects are typically counted among the professions. Why not add registrars to that list?

HUMAN SKILLS

Technical skills and knowledge are necessary to be a good registrar, but they are not sufficient. The human skills of communication, understanding, compassion, and listening are equally important to our work. Use these skills often; and if you don't have them, develop them. Be mindful of the tone of voice and the non-verbal cues you send in meetings or in one-on-one interactions. Listen actively to the student complaint or unreasonable faculty demand; don't interrupt; maintain eye contact; and nod appropriately (if you can). You may not agree or ultimately give in, but you will have demonstrated respect for the other person. If you are unable to act, provide a reasoned explanation, and describe the context in which your decision was made. Recently a student requested a waiver that was clearly a violation of academic policy. Rather than responding with "No, it's against the rules," I explained how the request created a moral dilemma for me: if I made an exception for him, how could I justify *not* making the same exception for other similarly situated students? I pointed out that the request was against school policy, but also against my personal sense of fairness and justice. He was disappointed in my decision, but I feel the discussion was as important as the outcome.

Two human characteristics critical to our work are integrity and accountability. Doing the right thing is important for everyone, but perhaps more so for a professional. A good academic leader cannot wish away a problem: you must assume responsibility for errors and take action. Critics will undoubtedly point fingers when things go wrong, but in my experience many will be impressed (sadly) if you take responsibility and correct a mistake you or someone in your office made. This applies also to staff problems. It is much easier to correct a data entry error or to implement a better process than dealing with a poor attitude or poor performance. When you encounter such a problem, act promptly and make your expectations clear. It's your job.

My view of the registrar's office has changed drastically over the years. It has gone from righteous defender of transcript integrity and enforcer of academic rules and regulations (indeed, the only one on campus, or so it sometimes seems) to service provider for faculty and students. I have worked hard to break the all-too-common feeling of dread and reluctance held by many of our "customers" when they think about the registrar's office, and I am fortunate to have worked at schools with small enough student and faculty populations to know some by name. My focus has shifted from FERPA, graduation planning, and room reservation software packages—certainly all important facets of the registrar's work—to people. I make a conscious effort every day to engage others personally and face-to-face, no small challenge in an age where instant electronic communication and 24/7 service is the norm. Long ago I implemented an "open door" policy. Most of these drop-in visits are work-related, and I appreciate how a short conversation can sometimes eliminate endless email exchanges. More gratifying, though, are the non-work related visits by students and faculty: "Oh nothing in particular, I was in the area and thought I would pop in to say hello." That is success.

A related word of advice to registrars in professional schools (*e.g.*, theology, dentistry, law, medicine), such as myself, who are untrained or unfamiliar with the discipline being taught. Make a special effort to visit classrooms, labs, clinics, and mock courtrooms to get a sense of what and how students learn and how faculty delivers content. In doing so, you demonstrate respect for the core enterprise of the school and open doors for conversation and relationship building with key customer groups. You also provide an opportunity for them to learn about you, what you do, and how your office fits into the functioning of the school. At the risk of sounding too Pollyanna, there is a practical value to these visits. I am now able to anticipate scheduling needs and room preferences for some courses, and have a deeper understanding of course sequencing and prerequisites.

GROWTH AND DEVELOPMENT

If you accept my challenge that the registrar is a developing profession, you acknowledge important characteristics of being a professional, including a commitment to lifelong development of yourself and of the profession. We play a critical role in identifying, mentoring, and growing the next generation of professional registrars.

Be constantly vigilant in identifying growth and development opportunities and take full advantage of them. It's worthwhile to think small and local in this regard, but don't forget about learning opportunities beyond your institution. Human resources offices at most schools coordinate seminars on "dealing with difficult people" or "conflict management," certainly two skills important to the registrar. Attend such seminars and actively encourage your staff to do so. It's important to demonstrate how much you value professional growth for everyone. Major SIS and room scheduling vendors (to name just two) offer an annual users conference, where important technical updates are shared and valuable contacts are made. Attend and take a staff member, if possible. It's important to stay current on advances in the tools of the profession. The jewel in the crown for us is AACRAO, its regional components, and the national meeting. Our professional organization has been invaluable to me, and it was primarily through my involvement that I began to develop as a registrar. I have gone from a mostly passive attendee at the annual meeting, to facilitator, committee member, presenter, and candidate for national office. *College and University* is one of a handful of professional, peer-reviewed journals I read regularly. I encourage you to become an active and lifelong participant.

I believe firmly in the value of formal learning and in what it contributes to personal and professional growth. There is no degree in "registrarial sciences," but a registrar should never discount the possibility of pursuing the next level of higher education. If you don't have a bachelor's degree, consider enrolling in a degree completion program for working professionals. If you have a bachelor's, think about pursuing a master's or doctoral degree. I returned to graduate school in 2000, and although it was difficult, I have not regretted it for a minute. The skills you build in an advanced degree program—critical thinking, teamwork, reflection, time management, communication, research—will serve you well in the profession. In the academic environment where we all work, an advanced degree carries cachet with faculty, and can build "street cred" with this important customer group. I don't believe it's entirely my imagination when at my institution I note a tinge of respect for *Dr.* Bender, who is regularly seen reading the peer-reviewed journal *College and University*, and who travels to national conferences to give formal presentations. How different that perception is from the one who hounds people for grades and demands justification for a simple change to the catalog description of a course.

Mentoring has its appropriate place in this skill set. For new registrars, I recommend you actively seek at least one mentor and hope you end up with many. Think broadly when choosing a mentor. It should be someone you admire, respect and trust, perhaps someone who has experience in the profession or at the institution. Do not limit yourself to selecting "the registrar" unless, however, the fit is right. There is only one registrar on campus, and if you don't get along with that person, look elsewhere. Remember, you are not looking for someone to train you for a job; you are looking for someone to help you grow and develop skills that will sustain your success. In retrospect, I wish I had been more proactive in this regard.

For established registrars who may be reading this essay, actively mentor a promising staff member. It's a fact that you are a role model (whether you want to be or not); your daily behavior, the decisions you make, and how you handle stressful situations and people send powerful messages about you as a leader. Being a mentor is slightly different, especially when it comes to developing the next generation of professionals. Be alert to the promising young staffer who has the right combination of skill sets to be a good registrar. Spend a little more time with that person, share a copy of

C&U or forward the weekly *Transcript* email. When the time is right, have a conversation about their career plans and ask them to think about becoming a registrar. Development professionals call it "The Ask," and it is powerful. I don't think anyone is born wanting to grow up to be a registrar. We should not leave the future of our profession to chance.

REFLECTION AND STRATEGIC THINKING

There is no denying that being a successful registrar requires a high level of proficiency in attention to detail, organization, time management, follow through, and technical skills. Managing people demands additional skills that a good registrar must also have. We are successful because of the ability to manage just such a workload. I know from experience how easy it is to get lost in the details of the day-to-day demands of a busy office, but I strongly recommend you make time for quiet reflection. "Turn it off" as often as you can and think strategically about large issues that could impact you, your work, your office, and the institution. Ask yourself: why has this been a problem for as long as anyone can remember, and is there something I can do to solve it? What is the next big issue in the profession (think electronic transcript exchange) and how does it play out at my school? What is the long range plan for this office and how does it support the mission of the university? There are important issues for the registrar beyond FERPA, and they require your attention.

The professional development activities described above are an obvious and rich source of new ideas and new thinking, and I reiterate how critical such engagement is to growing and expanding the profession. When flying home from a national meeting or driving home from work or class, give an idea freedom to bounce around your brain unrestricted. You could be surprised where it leads. Another important trigger to new ways of thinking is your professional reading. Don't set aside the latest edition of *College and University* or any journal you read regularly with the promise to pick it up later; there are too many distractions. If you find a few moments during the workday to read, make it a special event. Leave the office, have a cup of coffee, sit outside: there is nothing like no phone or foot traffic and no computer to force you to slow down and to give you the opportunity to engage in critical, reflective thought. It is some of the most important work you will do. Lastly, do not discard chance as a source of valuable new ideas. A conversation on an unrelated topic in a meeting, a book you are reading for pleasure, an interview you hear on the radio—such inputs can spur new thoughts related to your work and development. And by all means, do not attempt to schedule 20 minutes of "quiet reflection" twice a week! You cannot schedule spontaneity, creativity, or innovation. They happen organically.

CONCLUSION

Throughout your career, keep an eye on the future. Set clear, measurable short- and long-term goals for yourself, your office, and the profession. Regularly reflect and take stock of your progress. Keep in mind that your success will not be linear, but the overall trend should be positive. Always strive to be better: develop a new skill, design a new process or implement a new tool, read or do something that challenges you, and most importantly, promote and advance the *profession*.

3

CHAPTER THREE

The Inconspicuous Leader

MEREDITH BRAZ

It was the

end of a long work day: the door to the registrar's office was closed, and we were huddled over our desks appreciating the recent quiet. Some of us were attempting to untangle complex questions into simpler parts; a few of us were trying to complete some data entry without constant interruption; and I was making a final effort to answer a few more e-mails before heading home. Then came a knock at the door. Despite the looks of my staff as they silently begged "please don't," I opened the door reluctantly. There stood a student, registration card in hand. She darted inside and made it clear that she required immediate assistance. As I began to explain the registration procedure, she interrupted and proclaimed loudly, "No, I want to talk to her" as she pointed to the support staff member behind me who typically sits at the service area. To the student, I had no credibility; I was invisible. It made no difference to her that I had completely redesigned and implemented the entire registration system in detail. Thus it is with the registrar. Since then, students have said to me incredulously, "So there really *is* a registrar?" And so to all who "may be affected by skepticism and who do not believe except what they see," I say, "Yes, Virginia, there really *is* a registrar."

As a matter of fact, there are many hundreds if not thousands of registrars—unsung leaders in U.S. higher education who often may be "unseen" but who are both quite present and surprisingly influential. Leadership styles among us vary somewhat, but many of us practice what I call "inconspicuous" leadership. My strengths do not lie in my polished rhetoric or quick wit, in my ability to energize audiences, nor in my capacity to impress with grandiose accomplishments that make headlines; I confess that although I try my best—particularly when circumstances call for such abilities—others are much more skilled in these areas. Given the option, I shy away from the spotlight. I know my limitations and recognize that I must both partner with and learn from others who are more accomplished at "being visible." My strengths lie in my abilities to think globally and strategically; to garner confidence and respect; to keep my focus; and to build consensus so that goals are achieved. Like so many registrars, I don't get or seek a lot of attention; I just get things done.

As a leader, I constantly seek to cultivate my patience and deepen my confidence in my abilities while trying to express the genuine enjoyment and satisfaction I obtain from my work. I do this in the hope that others may be inspired to find gratification in their work as well. Doing work that fully engages us and that is naturally enriching is essential to good leadership. When we derive pleasure from the work we do, those around us are more likely not only to approach their work positively but also to be more fully engaged in it. First and foremost, a leader is a model who sets expectations for him—or herself—and, thus, for others.

When I achieve a goal (which never happens as a result of my efforts alone but always with the help of others), it is immensely satisfying. Typically, the registrar can anticipate the effects of her leadership initiatives; and often, the tendrils of a systems change are widespread and have a positive impact on a great many on our campuses. Breaking through barriers to change in order to move an institution forward is an art practiced over and over by registrars. In fact, sometimes the most effective way to lead is to intentionally *not* seek attention and so avoid a negative reaction. Change is not always embraced, and the outcome is what matters.

I have learned when to push others gently, so as to motivate, and when to step back and let things flow. Always, I keep the vision in focus and steer toward achievable goals. I don't do it perfectly by any means, and I have made many mistakes along the way. Nor am I unique: This is the reality of the leadership I see all around me when I connect with fellow registrars. In fact, they continually impress me with their ability to lead in increasingly complex academic environments and with their generous sharing of their expertise. A good leader always finds mentors (I have had many) who help them along the way; she also makes time to mentor others. One of the greatest pleasures is to see someone you have mentored enjoy success.

"Inconspicuous" is not the same as "silent" or "acquiescent." Leadership requires confidence, which, unfortunately, may on occasion be misconstrued by the insecure as self-importance or arrogance. Nevertheless, it is important to be confident about your expertise and not hesitate to share it with others. Senior officers should be confident in your leadership, and you should seek opportunities to build that confidence. Never underestimate the value of utilizing good management techniques and providing opportunities for staff input and independent work; yet the job of a leader should never be conflated with that of a manager. Almost any position in an organization can be a leadership position, and anyone can develop leadership ability from the start of their careers and within the constraints of any position. Potential for leadership often shows itself early; it can be nurtured in a support role, technical role, and managerial role as well as in a role at the level of director or above. Developing trust, planning strategically, and then taking action toward a focused vision are the cornerstones of my leadership style. At the same time, I seek to build connections, use imagination to inspire, and insist on excellence (not perfection, which is a different thing altogether).

There are many ways in which the registrar is a natural leader even as she is forced by virtue of the position to be one. The registrar never works alone, and she must remain focused on the institutional vision even as the institution grows and changes and as projects are implemented. To do this effectively, we must continually make and cultivate connections both within and outside the institution. We partner with many, and we often help bring others' visions to fruition. We cannot avoid challenges; they come our way daily, so we become adept at meeting them head on, even when they are uncomfortable. A tension inherent in our position is that we are respected though not necessarily always liked; this can prove difficult for some leaders. We implement projects continuously, and to do so we have to be focused and goal oriented. Our daily experiences help us build resilience, a particular asset during times of budget cuts. And because we hold a position that is central to our institution's operations, we are adept at seeing the "big picture." All of these are essential elements of good leadership. The registrar develops these skills as a foundation of the profession, distinct from other equally necessary technical and managerial skill sets. Finally, the registrar is a natural leader because he has no choice but to develop a good sense of humor. Who else hears the most outrageous excuses, sees the most extreme behaviors, or is asked to accomplish what is so laughable?

Why, then, do so many registrars not believe themselves to be influential institutional leaders? Students, campus colleagues, and friends typically respond respectfully when we tell them that our title is "registrar;" yet few know the entirety of what we do. Perhaps it is how leadership is often defined, or maybe we need to assess and strengthen our leadership roles and envision how our role can contribute even more to the campus environment. I suggest the following:

- Value what you do: It all begins here. Question any assumptions you or others have that what you provide as a leader is anything but essential and remarkable. Insist on being a leader.
- Borrow shamelessly, and give generously. We are a collection of leaders who share openly in a multitude of ways. Connect, and recognize the strength we give one another in this important role. Connect as well with leaders from other professions, and learn from and use their skills to supplement your own.
- Value goal achievement over credit: It is wonderful to be recognized, but the sheer complexity of campus initiatives often requires letting go of individual accolades. When initiatives are successful, relish the fact that you have achieved your goal, and be sure to celebrate.
- Come into the limelight once in a while: It is important to make others aware of your value and of your contributions to the institution. If self-promotion or office PR is not your strength, learn techniques for communicating your message, and partner with those who are good at it. Important people need to recognize you and your work. Be comfortable with being inconspicuous as well as present—and, perhaps, visible—where and when it matters.
- Cultivate endless patience: Plan; think and reflect deliberately; understand and accept what those you are leading can and cannot accept; and help them as best as you are able. Be prepared to be disappointed—quite regularly, in fact—and keep moving forward regardless.
- Develop a strong support system outside of work: It is said by many—and I agree—that having friends outside of work,

engaging in exercise, pursuing hobbies, and keeping a healthy work/life balance are important. Stressed-out people do not make good leaders.

- Enjoy what you do: Have fun! If you don't find yourself laughing frequently and looking forward to going to work, then the position is not a good fit. You cannot lead well if you are not having fun.

The registrar, while often an inconspicuous leader, is not unremarkable; in fact, quite the opposite is true. On occasion, someone actually does see us and what we do as leaders serving our institutions. When that happens, it makes us truly glad. *Alas, how dreary would be the world if there were no registrars.*

4

CHAPTER FOUR

Mentoring the Next Generation of Leaders

SHARON F. CRAMER

As members

of enrollment management units look ahead to the next few years, they anticipate many institution-wide challenges: implementation of a new student information system, major upgrade of an existing system, or re-configuring an existing system to reflect changes in academic policies or to accommodate new federal or state guidelines. Many of these prospective changes elicit dread—of consequent drains on basic operations, of pressures on staff, of the implications of testing new systems, and of the pressure to be "error free." This article encourages enrollment management supervisors to view these "exceptional circumstances" in a new way: as "greenhouses" for facilitating the development of leadership perspectives and as unique opportunities for mentoring. This article also is intended to serve as a resource for enrollment management staff members who might consider taking on more responsibilities—and perhaps, eventually, leadership roles within (and beyond) their current positions/departments.

In 1999, I was asked to serve as executive director of our campus transition from a home-grown, back-office product to a commercially developed, web-based student information system. The team of enrollment management members assigned to the project worked closely with information technology staff, campus members, and administrators. The result was a cultural change on our campus that prepared all of us to better adjust not only to that initial implementation but also to many subsequent changes (*e.g.*, implementation of another student information system, change of product for our learning management and degree audit systems). Our experiences inspired *Student Information Systems: A Guide to Implementation Success* (Cramer 2005) as well as a chapter in Haab and Cramer's (2011) *Technology Integration in Higher Education: Social and Organizational Aspects* on the systemic aspects of such changes.

Although my experience with a full-time team is my reference point for this article, enrollment management professionals and supervisors can use my recommendations at any point in an annual cycle. Most enrollment management departments can utilize the ideas in this article for responsibilities that have a defined start, middle, and end (*e.g.*, semester registration, communication about a new student registration or faculty grading procedure), as well as for technology implementations such as those mentioned above.

The thesis of this article is that mentoring is one of the unique opportunities that arise in the process of working on small or large "exceptional projects." Ideally, as Norton and Kaplan (2004) suggest, an institution's strategic plan will connect with the performance programs of enrollment management professionals. The following questions may be asked either by the person who will serve as a mentor or by the person who seeks to become a leader.

- *Question 1*: What can a mentor do to create a climate supportive of leadership aspirations and opportunities?
- *Question 2*: How can new challenges become self-evaluative opportunities?
- *Question 3*: How does one make the transition from learner to mentor or leader?

Consideration of each of these questions is designed to stimulate further conversation. Ideally, given the relative scarcity and high cost of formal mentoring programs—and the many opportunities for (and low cost of) informal ones—this article also may stimulate a commitment to informal mentoring relationships. Although not every supervisor can be an effective mentor (and not every supervisee can become a leader), this article may inspire you to think differently about yourself and those with whom you work.

MENTORING PRAGMATICS: GIVING AND GETTING

For the most part, enrollment management specialists have in-depth knowledge of and experience with specific tasks in their day-to-day work. They familiarize themselves with the responsibilities required to perform their jobs. Often, this means that their only work contacts are within their own offices. And although attendance at regional, state, or national professional conferences is a typical expectation at some campuses, many enrollment management professionals retire without ever meeting their counterparts at other institutions—or even on their own campus. Intentional planning for leadership experiences can be accomplished either within a campus or beyond it.

Question 1: What can a mentor do to create a climate supportive of leadership aspirations and opportunities?

Confidence and the ability to solve problems are essential aspects of leadership. These skills are best cultivated in a climate of candor and self-reflective examination about what is working and what needs to be improved. Self-reflection is a habit that individuals can learn as they observe others who routinely strive to ensure that evolving solutions match identified problems. Members of my project team told me that as a result of their participation, they began to see themselves in new ways. Although our project had no explicit leadership development component, several team members have since been promoted to positions of leadership. Their project experiences helped them identify new aspirations and attain personal and professional transformations. As they learned more about the interconnections among different aspects of enrollment management, information technology, and other campus efforts, the silos within which they had worked began to be replaced by cross-campus awareness and relationships. As team members returned at the end of the project to their previous positions, many realized that what previously had been a comfortable employment fit no longer was.

The challenges our team sought to address proved to be the "machines" that tore down "work silos" during the project. Routines were no more. Exceptional circumstances—really, short-term leadership assignments—proved to be opportunities for enrollment management specialists to confront problems they had not previously encountered. They had to learn to adjust to ambiguity. Suddenly, strategies on which they had relied were not relevant to the problems they faced. Although not every supervisee—nor every member of a full-time team—had the potential to become a leader, all needed to be encouraged to rise to their individual levels of excellence. It fell to the supervisors to help them accomplish tasks they had thought were beyond their ability.

Helping enrollment management specialists to overcome their apprehension and become adaptive, creative problem solvers requires that supervisors/mentors:

- Believe in their supervisees: They will gain confidence because they know their mentors believe in them.
- Listen to them as they verbalize their thoughts, and then provide gentle direction.
- Give them access to resources on and off campus.

- Create a learning organization such that all participate in shared problem-solving.
- Provide honest feedback during supervisory sessions, the goal being to facilitate leadership development.

At a particularly difficult juncture in our project, I expressed my hopelessness to our executive sponsor, the vice president of finance and management. His response was to ask me if I thought the newly elected president (it was shortly after a national election) was fully informed about all aspects of running the nation. He encouraged me to do what the president likely was doing: surrounding himself with smart, thoughtful, articulate people and reflecting on the information they provided before taking action. I was reassured to know that my mentor was aware of the gaps in my knowledge. The conversation went a long way toward helping me to keep the project moving ahead—and to ensuring my own professional growth.

At crucial points, I utilized different strategies to give project team members opportunities to build their skills. When we felt perplexed by the task of communicating with campus members, we developed a communication plan. Whole-team discussions involved a variety of campus experts in its design. We have continued to use the paradigms we developed. For example, recent use of a campus researcher, information technology specialist, and representatives from campus governance and enrollment management led to recommendations for a policy regarding the use of technology rather than a narrowly defined decision-making process to address an advisement problem during registration.

Prior to their involvement in the project, many team members had viewed complex outcomes as emerging from behind closed doors. (In a similar way, people who dine at a sophisticated restaurant witness only the presentation of an elaborate entrée; the waiter's flourish gives no hint of what was involved in creating the dish).

In fact, deconstructing leadership may be likened to watching the Food Network: certain routines for problem solving become clear. Much like learning to dice an onion, previously unknown ideas and skills (*e.g.*, cross training, learning the jargon of different campus units) can be demystified. An example of this for our team was sharing "annual reports." Most enrollment management professionals never saw the department or unit annual reports. Sharing them with team members gave them insights into what was shared with the executive sponsor of the project and also served as a point of pride. This helped them understand aspects of the enterprise of which they previously were unaware.

Opportunities to use one's knowledge in campus-wide contexts can facilitate increased confidence and skills. Giving individuals titles (*e.g.*, project manager, coordinator) for specific exceptional circumstances or for short-term implementations can facilitate leadership development. Additional graduated leadership opportunities include the following:

- Participating in leadership-oriented professional development activities (online, on and/or off campus);
- Serving as "lead" on a committee (*e.g.*, conference room pilots of new procedures, discussion of policy matters) composed of enrollment management specialists as well as other campus members; and
- Presenting periodic work-related updates by presenting at campus, state, and/or national conferences.

Ideally, these new experiences will enable enrollment management professionals to build their confidence and develop a new sense of self. Note, however, that assistance may be needed to foster some employees' willingness to move beyond the comfort zone of familiar routines.

Question 2: How can new challenges become self-evaluative opportunities?

As exceptional circumstances come to be seen as incubators for learning, enrollment management specialists are likely to become increasingly self-reflective. Rather than perceiving corrections or recommendations for reconsiderations as criticism or personal attacks, enrollment management professionals may come to perceive them instead as opportunities for self-improvement. Whereas I had previously completed annual performance evaluations, I asked each team member to prepare a self-evaluation. I also asked them to give me anonymous, specific feedback on my leadership goals; they then had the opportunity to see how I responded. Many since have let me know that it was what I *did* rather than what I *said* that helped them understand professional evolution as essential. Ideally, identifying explicit leadership opportunities for the year ahead and building them into annual reviews will help ensure that these activities take place. Linking the actions with the unit's (or the college's) strategic plan can facilitate increased understanding of how the work of the enrollment management unit affects the campus as a whole.

Consider these opportunities to develop leadership skills during exceptional circumstances:

- Incorporate specific skills into annual reviews that can be used during the exceptional circumstance as well as thereafter.
- Facilitate participation in broad-based training experiences.
- Take ten minutes every Thursday afternoon to ask:
  - "What did I do to help my leadership candidates stretch beyond their reach?"
  - "How did I recognize efforts as well as achievements?"
  - "What happened this week to show me that progress is being made toward leadership as well as toward the specific goals of the exceptional circumstance?"

As a project team, we participated in two retreats each year that were designed to help us think in new ways about ourselves and our work. One retreat focused on the team described by Ken Blanchard et. al (2000) in *High Five*. The book uses a parable to illustrate how teamwork requires not only one or two outstanding talents but also capacity for improvement by all members. A light-hearted starting point for discussion, the book clarified ways in which team members could support one anothers' developing skills and thereby learn more about themselves. As we learned together, all team members grew in their confidence as well as in their skill set.

Question 3: How does one make the transition from learner to mentor or leader?

One aspect of making the transition from learner to leader involves increased awareness of and comfort level with others on campus. Intentionally incorporating campus-wide activities into performance programs can facilitate this process. Consider, for example, the following:

- Participate in campus-wide committees to consider challenges and benefits likely to be derived during/after resolution of the exceptional circumstance.
- Serve on a campus governance committee that oversees policies pertinent to the exceptional circumstance.
- Join a listserv sponsored by the vendor, a users' group associated with the product, or a professional organization.

Just as becoming a leader is not an option for everyone, so becoming a mentor is not an option for every supervisor. Some supervisors have little or no capacity for leadership or mentoring. This includes supervisors who have no interest in investing their time and energy in others, who are poor at self-reflection, and who are loath to leave old habits behind. If you are a potential leader and realize that your supervisor is ill-suited to mentor you, then consider others who may be resources. Similarly, if you are a supervisor and recognize that one of your direct reports has the capacity for leadership *but you are not the right mentor,* then explore other ways in which your campus might provide mentoring to this individual. Candid recognition of impediments to mentoring can minimize (if not eliminate) wasted time and effort.

The following questions may aid potential leaders and mentors as they consider the transition from learner to leader:

- What capabilities do I already possess that could serve as the basis of mentoring or leading?
- Which aspects of my professional and educational background could provide the foundation for further learning in the area of mentoring or leadership? In what areas would I need to develop new frames of reference and greater depth of knowledge?
- Am I willing and able to participate in self-reflective inquiry, adjustment, and forward thinking to develop my mentoring or leadership skills ?
- Who could serve as professional resources for me as I develop my mentoring or leadership skills? What is the best way to invite these individuals to assist me as I develop?
- How can I develop the skill set I believe to be essential to the mentor or leader I aspire to be?
- What supports are necessary for me to take reasonable risks in my professional development as a mentor or leader?

CONCLUSION

Exceptional circumstances for enrollment management staff members should be perceived as "greenhouses" for facilitating the development of leadership perspectives and as unique opportunities for mentoring. Greenhouses can be both cloying and useful; the moisture and heat can be oppressive. But if you recognize that time in the greenhouse is short and that it facilitates desirable outcomes, then the discomfort may be perceived as worthwhile.

Prospective Leaders: Leadership is not just for other people. Consider what you might contribute to your department and/or to your campus. Take advantage of opportunities to learn whether leadership could be a satisfying addition to your career.

Prospective Mentors: The tendency in exceptional circumstances is to hope they pass quickly, with as little "skin loss" as possible. Instead, seek to perceive them as opportunities for learning and growth. As future leaders begin to view their work, campus, and profession in new ways, they begin as well to consider how they might take on new roles. Supervisors can assist with this process. As one team member said, "I saw through the mirage I'd been in before: there were opportunities in front of me that I'd never previously considered."

Acknowledgments: Many thanks to the following Buffalo State colleagues for their helpful assistance with this article: Judi Basinski, Connie Cooke, Leslie Dixie-Smith, Don Erwin, Stan Kardonsky, Heather Maldonado, and Colleen Sullivan.

5

CHAPTER FIVE

Learning to Lead

HANSFORD M. EPES

Many

dedicated people enter our profession intentionally and carefully. Then there are the rest of us. My venturing into the world of the registrar came through a phone call from the academic dean, also a good friend: "The registrar's leaving. Would you take over as interim registrar?" The choice seemed felicitous: I had long experience as a faculty advisor and as a department and program chair; a certain level of facility with information technology and with issues of study abroad; and I was a tenured member of a department perceived as overstaffed. So, after 35 years on the Davidson faculty, I took over as registrar—and wound up staying, not as interim, but for another dozen years as registrar—while still teaching a class each semester. (I wouldn't have accepted without continuing to teach, a vocation that I genuinely love.)

I saw the opportunity as precisely that, deciding rather quickly that despite no formal preparation whatsoever for the job, I could bring some strengths to it—especially with an office staff in place that collectively had many years of experience.

And I knew two things: one was that I needed to learn; the other, that I needed to lead. After a while, I realized that they were not two things, but two sides of the same thing. Give me a few more pages, and perhaps I can clarify that assertion.

Let me pause for a little background. Davidson College is a highly selective four-year baccalaureate college. Our students represent entirely what we call the traditional age, 18–22; all are full-time, and all are residential. A large majority will aspire to and achieve education beyond the bachelor's degree at graduate and professional schools throughout the United States and elsewhere. Tuition is high, although donor generosity means that financial aid is relatively abundant. High tuition does, however, encourage both students and their parents to expect a comparably high level of service. Even that brief outline should alert anyone that the registrar's challenges at Davidson match only in part those faced by colleagues in our rich variety of colleges and universities.

Some aspects of the profession, however, do confront just about all of us. To begin with, a registrar—especially a new one—needs to learn a great number of things. We might be able to collect them into three categories. If this were a presentation, the three categories would demand either an acronym or alliteration. I'll settle for the latter and gather what I needed to learn into headings: Procedures, Politics, and People. The procedures, obviously, are the office routines and the needs behind them, along with the mechanisms (such as software) that support those routines and needs. The politics are largely but not exclusively local: how we develop procedures to the needs of others on the campus and beyond—and what institutional avenues and structures make the registrar's office effective in simultaneously preserving routine and in facilitating change. People underlie both of those categories, of course: procedures exist, after all, to serve the needs of people; and institutional structures for governance are not really mere charts, but the people named within them. Moreover, and crucially, any office itself consists of people expecting leadership and collegiality.

I decided early on that it would be useful for me to learn at least the basics of our student information system (Banner). One person within the office, involved in the original installation, had exemplary knowledge about the information system itself, a strong sense of how what we did within it related to the work of others, and a great deal of patience in teaching me what it could and couldn't do. Others on staff were skilled at using the software to accomplish tasks that traditionally had fallen to them, although I concluded that some cross-training in those tasks would be a reasonable priority not merely for the general effectiveness of the office, but because continued learning could and should help everyone avoid the stultifying consequences of unchanging routine. I wanted to know how it all worked, not just to provide a sense of how long a task should take, or how complex it might be, but frankly because I enjoy that sort of learning. In the process, and over time, I learned the downside of cross-training—being reminded on occasion that a task that becomes everyone's responsibility becomes no one's. Were I to start over, I'd be more aware of the dangers of trying to move away from "her job" toward "our job;" that formulation is appropriate, but may not communicate individual expectations well.

As luck would have it, I came into the registrar's office at the time Banner moved strongly toward self-service for both students and faculty. With the support of our information technology department, we quickly went about taking advantage of that new direction. Doing so took us away from adding terminals and temporary data entry assistance during drop/add and away from bubble sheets, #2 pencils, and optical scanners for grade entry. We invested some effort in showing faculty members how to enter grades on the computer rather than filling in paper sheets—and found the new procedure almost universally welcomed as faculty members quickly learned how to do it. Of course, faculty being as we are, there was one senior professor who brought his grades to the office in order, in his words, "to protest the spread of technology." Oblivious to the irony of his action, he brought them in on a bubble sheet.

Fortunately, as well, the campus embarked at roughly the same time on use of data warehousing. Rather than trying to anticipate questions and have experts at IT write programs to answer them, we worked with IT to develop tables, and we all learned how to produce simple queries using Microsoft Access. I even wound up writing an Access report to audit senior completion of general graduation requirements. A few other MS Access reports replaced some of the items the office had been using for years. What I learned in that process was how to use Access, certainly—but much more importantly, how much people in the office enjoyed learning even at an elementary level how to use new tools to accomplish old tasks.

Politics can suggest a number of things, but I'll use the word in the broadest possible sense: negotiating the eccentricities of both the local and broader communities that have a reasonable stake in what the registrar's office does and learning how to exert, or at least understand, influence within those communities. As a longtime faculty member, at least I had the advantage of already knowing everyone and being able to get to anyone rather directly; and I knew the local politics well. (In the words of the then college president: "Hansford knows where the bodies are buried, and probably buried some of them himself.")

The wider community presented a different challenge. The registrar must also live in the world of law, of accreditation, and the like. Not having the advantage of coming from a program in higher education administration, I had not been through one of the standard courses: legal issues in higher education. Knowing no more about FERPA than the average faculty member—which means not much—I welcomed eagerly the support provided by AACRAO through both publications and extensive presentations at conferences. That support, supplemented by contacts with colleagues at other institutions, became my cram course about the wider community in legal and other ways. It helped with office efficiency (and sustainable practices) when we concluded we could cease filing, on paper, every student request to have transcripts sent to a grad school or a study abroad program. It helped when we decided to quit sending semester grade reports automatically to parents, because it enabled me (among other things) to clarify for them the difference between stipulating what a college may do and what it must do. Of course, many parents still were unsettled by the policy. During panel discussions for parents at orientation, the issue continued to arise—and I tried humorously to poke fun at the extreme decisions of bureaucrats while defending, in good conscience, the principle behind both FERPA and our decisions relative to it. (I did cut back on poking fun at bureaucrats when one mother of a new freshman expressed interest in my snide comments about the FERPA bureaucracy—and introduced herself as the Secretary of Education.)

The wider political context does remind us, however, that our responsibilities as registrars extend beyond the edges of our campus and even that our professionalism can demand on occasion that we stand our ground against our own faculties and administrations. I cannot help noticing in media accounts of occasional scandals about grades and credentials how seldom a registrar is mentioned, and I take that as a sign of campuses on which the registrar has been relegated to a role lacking the respect and the influence that the office must have. When deans of various sorts have been implicated in grade changes or questionable regulations, it's not hard to figure out that campus politics have impeded the registrar's responsibility—and hence that of the campus—to the wider community.

People present the biggest challenge, in part because there is so much to learn in the attempt to meet that challenge. We can read and hear a great deal about leadership (which certainly implies leading people) and about managing, and we can take grateful note of the many who observe that while leadership and management may have much in common, they are not the same thing at all. Unfortunately for my snobbish stylistic tastes, much of what we read and hear hides both insights and truisms under writing of the sort that assumes useful concepts arise from converting nouns into adjectives or verbs, from removing human subjects from as many sentences as possible, and from overusing admirable terms until they have all the uplift of a three-day old balloon. (I suspect I can live happily for several years without ever again reading or hearing "innovation" or "excellence.")

Of course, I've just illustrated—deliberately—why someone coming from a faculty background might have held positions of responsibility while learning little about managing others. We often don't manage well because we're bound to our own academic and stylistic convictions—and we aren't managed readily for the same reason.

So I was led under protest—and not too effectively—to concede the value of such genuinely productive managerial insights as the importance of establishing goals that are smart: specific, measurable, attainable, and the rest.

But part of my protest persists: leadership requires smart management, to be sure—but it's something far greater.

And that's where I sum up a dozen years, at a career's end, spent as a registrar: "learning to lead" means more than just learning what it takes to lead an office, to master its procedures, or to respect its role in both smaller and larger communities.

The phrase "learning to lead" suggests, for me, that the act of learning is itself an act of leadership. I had a great advantage: I came into an office knowing less than others with whom I worked every day. Learning from them made me demonstrate respect for them. Learning with them allowed us together to respond to changes because we could understand, together, that learning something different was an opportunity, not a threat. Perhaps someone whose vocation was learning itself could, by example, be an effective leader precisely because of that vocation.

What could be a better model in education, after all? Learning involves three directions: mastering the past, questioning the present, and suggesting the new. Helping to create that climate in an office that provides professional and essential support for education might have been a good day's work. Or a good twelve years.

6

CHAPTER SIX

A Leader with Unexpected Roots

SUSAN GOTTHEIL

I am a

child of the sixties...True, I did not "come of age" until the 70s but I am a baby boomer none the less. I proudly marched in anti-war demonstrations and was even prouder that "my country" stayed out of Vietnam and that we re-created underground railroads to help young American boys escape the draft. I grew up in Montreal (Quebec) during the Quiet Revolution—when the whole society rebelled against the patriarchal church, and social justice values and principles became embedded in provincial and even federal politics. Canadians were early adopters of Medicare and were not ashamed of offering a "social safety net" to help those who lost their jobs or became ill or disabled. After the Second World War, we opened our country to immigrants and refugees (although the shuttering of those doors to Jews and others trying to escape Nazi Europe has remained a dark spot in our collective history) and proclaimed ourselves a "multicultural" society. We smugly believed that the race issues exploding on the streets of the States were not our problem.

Yet it was not long after I started my postsecondary studies that my complacency was shaken and my analytical tools honed. Education opened my eyes to the world around me. Canadian industry was part of the military-industrial complex and complicit in manufacturing napalm that killed and maimed thousands of innocent people. Many children were living in poverty in my hometown. Although French-speaking Quebecers were in the majority in our province, the language of business remained English and many francophones dropped out of high school and remained in low paying jobs and out of the halls of power. If Native (Aboriginal) Canadians were in anyone's consciousness at all it was as a stereotype—living in teepees on the Prairies or in igloos with dogsleds in the far North (not in nearby communities or dispossessed of their land and living in communities without adequate food, shelter and water). As a young woman, I realized that I faced blatant and systemic discrimination, and unless things changed I would not have the same opportunities as my male peers to intellectually grow and develop and contribute to society—never mind being paid equally. The seeds of rebellion were sown.

CHANGING THE SYSTEM FROM WITHIN

I became a student activist on campus—establishing a Woman's Centre and helping friends start a GLBT bookstore, protesting the destruction of old Victorian mansions in nearby neighborhoods, studying the writings of Karl Marx and Mao Tse Tung, and trying to imagine a more utopian and egalitarian world in which to live. Many debates ensued over strong coffee and beer—could the world be changed through evolutionary shifts in policy and processes, or were more radical, revolutionary tactics necessary? My pacifist nature led to rifts in friendships as I declared my unease with violent actions (that were never acted upon) against "the state."

Instead, I serendipitously found myself in a summer job at the Dean of Students Office researching the status of women (students, staff and faculty) on campus—and had my first career mentor set me on my journey of postsecondary work. Erin, a professor in the Faculty of Religious Studies, was a former nun who had embraced liberation theology and worked for many years with impoverished communities in South America. She was also a strong feminist. Nun, feminist, social activist, professor—these all seemed to me to be distinct roles, and I certainly couldn't fathom how anyone (except perhaps the Berrigan brothers in the United States who were pivotal in the anti-Nixon era) could mold what I considered disparate and contradictory traits into one personality. Yes, people are complex and complicated. Most importantly, I learned from Erin that one can be an effective agent of change and impact the lives of others by working *within* institutions. It was not necessary to blow them up.

"WE'RE BEHIND YOU": THE YOUNGER SIBLING COMPLEX

My educational journey took me to the United States where I could enroll in a graduate degree in women's history (Canada had no such programs at the time). Although my interest was in Canadian oral history I was told in no uncertain terms that I could not study Canadian history. The not-so-subtle message was that we were not worthy of study and no one really cared. So European history it was—and my fellow students rewarded me with a convocation present of an American flag with a 51st star added to it—a jocular message to let me know that they liked me despite my Canadian "second-class" citizenship.

Back in Canada I followed a circuitous career path—always passionate about what I was doing and convinced that I was making a difference. I taught humanities and women's studies for nine years in a college that served a diverse population of students, many of whom were immigrant and first-generation Canadians. I jumped careers and worked as an employment and educational equity officer at a university in a new city, pulling a husband and young family along with me. And when the opportunity came along to apply for a position of Assistant Vice President in student and academic services, I convinced myself I had the skills and abilities to lead a large team. Reflecting back to that period of my life I realize that I didn't know how much I didn't know. But it was my second career mentor, the provost, who took a chance and gave me the opportunity to bring my equity vision into the realm of student affairs.

It was at this juncture that the postsecondary world in Canada underwent cataclysmic shifts—large cuts in provincial funding and big tuition increases, the introduction of the *Macleans* university rankings, increased competitiveness, and the genteel "Canadian" approach to collaboration between universities gone. The university I worked for saw a 45 percent decline in enrollment over a five-year period. Our new president asked me to take the lead in working with colleagues across the university to turn things around. How could I say no? I have always been up for a challenge.

Being an academic at heart, I read up on best practices in student recruitment and retention, picked up tips at workshops in the States offered by consulting firms, and started attending AACRAO's Strategic Enrollment Management (SEM) Conference. I imported a strategic management framework into Canada and was quick to let colleagues know we were far behind our American friends in how we did business. In retrospect, I realize I was typically Canadian—feeling like a country cousin to big city-slickers. Perhaps I was still impacted by my graduate school experience. It took me some time to learn that Canadians are not "less than" or "behind" Americans. What works in one jurisdiction may not work in another. And sometimes those who leap too quickly can't catch themselves as they tumble over the edge. The Canadian educational system has been shaped by a different history and set of values and is governed by a different legislative system. Study your options, and do your research. Continually learn. Don't be afraid to innovate. But keep your eyes wide open.

WORDS OF THE WISE: GANDHI'S DICTUM

So I became a leader in Canadian strategic enrolment management. ("Who, me?") With more than 30 years now under my belt leading teams and change within postsecondary institutions, there are a few wise words I can pass on. Most of these can be found in the myriad of (other) books published on work, management, and leadership. Be true to yourself. Follow your passion(s). Admit your mistakes. Share the glory.

It is true that my success as a leader in SEM has been in my ability to continually see "the big picture," to inspire others to buy into the "change" I envisioned and was excited about, to understand the interconnectedness of different parts of the organization and the importance of working together, and to keep students at the center of all I do. But the most important lesson I have learned is that change does not happen in a vacuum, and no leader leads alone.

> *"I suppose leadership at one time meant muscles; but today it means getting along with people."*
>
> —MAHATMA GANDHI

Good leaders are fundamentally people who like other people. At least, I do. What has made me a successful enrollment management leader has been building partnerships and breaking down departmental silos in the institutions I have worked. It is true that I have also had to be analytical and strategic, recognizing that there are limited hours in the day and that priorities must be set if goals are to be achieved. ("Keep your eye on the prize.") However all the leaders I know have an innate sense of curiosity about the world around them and respect for the diverse people who live in it.

Leaders want to make a difference. Sometimes that means being a rebel, speaking up against inequities and injustices, and working to change "the system." It may also mean taking risks and not being afraid of failure or making mistakes. But no matter what, true leaders want to share their knowledge and passion, mentoring colleagues and students so they, too, may make a difference in the lives of others.

Do not follow where the path may lead.
Go instead where there is no path and leave a trail.

—HAROLD R. MCALINDON (ALSO ATTRIBUTED TO EMERSON AND OTHERS)

CHAPTER SEVEN

My Management Epiphanies (Don't Wait as Long for Yours!)

KAREN P. GUALTIER

I never

planned to work at a college, but I find I am vice president of student development at a community college; I served previously as assistant to the dean of academic services, as registrar, and as dean of enrollment management. I started my career in health care administration, and my master's was in public administration, so my only higher education experience was as a student and graduate research assistant. Consequently, I started every new position in the community college with a sense of "Oh no, what have I done? I really don't know anything about _____!" Over the years, that blank has been filled with such topics as legacy system conversions, FERPA, supervising clerical and professional staffs, faculty loading, optical imaging, commencement ceremonies, admissions, enrollment management, student involvement, disability services—the list goes on.

I survived my own ignorance by treating those topics as if they were subjects to be learned by reading files, books, and articles; attending conferences; contacting experts at other colleges who were willing to explain things; and applying the critical thinking skills that are the hallmark of a college education. Lately, however, I have realized that the key to success in higher education administration is not only learning subjects but also consistently applying some basic management strategies. Thinking through those strategies led to four epiphanies:

MODELING IS MORE THAN LOOKING GOOD

The adage "Lead by example" is accurate. Your staff will learn more from the attitude and behavior you model than they will from anything you include in a procedures manual, memo, or training seminar. While all of those things are important, none is as fundamental as the type of worker you are.

Are the phones ringing off the hook because the office is short staffed? Answer a phone. Is the line for a particular service long during the first week of classes? Stop and do triage: See if you can answer simple questions, or direct students to the office or person they really need to see. Is the brochure rack empty and every clerk working with students? Fill the rack. Did a department representative fail to show up at an open house, and prospective students are asking about the program? Man the department's table. Are these things your job? No, and they shouldn't be your ongoing responsibility. But if everyone is working hard and simply can't do anything more, help, regardless of the task. *When you do whatever it takes to make the program better, the wait shorter, or the process smoother, you are modeling the behavior you expect from your staff.*

But don't think that only your actions need to be modeled. How you acknowledge successes and failures is also critical. A manager who is quick to blame someone else for mistakes but takes all the credit for successes sets a very poor tone for subordinates. In that kind of atmosphere, no one wants to be responsible for anything because she will pay for it if anything goes wrong, and she will get no benefit if it turns out well. Staff tend to "hide" their mistakes, so that what could have been handled in relatively short order can mushroom into a disaster. *So admit when you are wrong, ask your staff for suggestions, and reverse or modify a decision you made if that is the right thing to do.*

Finally, praise and recognition are not finite commodities to be hoarded. If someone on your staff is responsible for a project's success, tell the world! A competent, well-respected staff makes you look good, and citing their names in reports to management, at staff meetings, or at faculty gatherings makes them want to continue to do good work. If you work with a colleague on a project that is successful, be sure to give her credit for what she has done, or at least acknowledge her contribution in a general way. *Giving credit when it is due demonstrates that you are confident enough in your abilities to share the stage.*

TALENT SCOUTS AND CASTING DIRECTORS AREN'T ONLY IN HOLLYWOOD

On rare occasions, you may be so fortunate as to have enough staff, each qualified to do his job. Or, if you are like most of us, that will never happen. (Wishing it were so will not help you; it will only drive you crazy!) Your only alternative is to carefully consider the talent that is available, and recognize that everyone (excepting perhaps the hardcore under-performer whom you should be trying to fire) has a talent of some sort. The person who has terrible interpersonal skills may be a good data entry operator; the professional who really doesn't like working with faculty or students may have the technical skills to query the database and work through the problems that inevitably accompany SIS releases and patches.

Then consider the work that needs to be done. While you must bear in mind the basic tenets of "position descriptions," there is wiggle room even in unionized environments—especially if you have more than one employee in a particular job category . Focus on the tasks rather than the positions, and try to match the tasks to the talent pool you have. Make adjustments gradually, and be sure that everyone understands that any changes in what they are doing are because they have the skill set required for their new task. If you keep the changes consistent with the type of work your staff are paid to do, they usually will respond positively. (After all, you are recognizing their talent and asking for their help!) In most cases, people are good at something because they enjoy it. So aligning work with staff members' strengths tends to make them happier over the long term.

Differentiate the staff member who quickly and competently completes assignments from the staff member who takes all day (or longer!) to complete a project so she will look too busy to have to do something else. An employee who isn't afraid to try something new or even to make a decision has the makings of a good manager. Find ways to mentor and reward her.

CUT YOUR LOSSES

Even the best manager makes bad decisions. Given the information available at the time, you made what clearly seemed the right decision—perhaps to revise a procedure, recommend a new policy, or hire someone to fill a position. But new information often comes into play, unexpected consequences arise, or the world's greatest candidate during the interview cannot deliver what he promised. Everyone understands that these things happen. *As long as this does not routinely happen to you*, you can turn the situation around by analyzing what went wrong and taking corrective measures.

There is no standard time frame you should allocate to a project or an employee before admitting that changes need to be made. On the one hand, be careful that you don't have a knee-jerk reaction to everything that goes wrong; if you do, you will be changing your mind so often that staff will become confused, and you'll gain a reputation for being unfocused. On the other hand, do not let your need to be right or to save face keep you wedded to a course of action that clearly is not working.

For projects and procedures, determine whether the concept or the execution was the source of the failure. If the concept was poor, then allowing additional time will not make things better. If the execution was poor but the concept basically sound, then time and minor adjustments may be sufficient to salvage the situation. Cut your losses more quickly on bad concepts than on bad executions.

A similar situation exists for "bad hires." If the problem with the new employee is one that training or mentoring can remedy, then take the time to work with the person. However, if the person cannot get along with anyone, cannot complete a project, or repeatedly makes bad decisions even though you have clearly explained ways in which she needs to improve her performance, then cut your losses quickly! Not only is the employee not getting the job done, but she also is hurting your reputation as a manager and making the work environment unpleasant (at best) and unproductive (at worst) for others.

DON'T LET THEM TAKE YOU HOSTAGE

One of the first things you should consider as a new manager is sitting with everyone you supervise to find out what it is they do. Learn how to process an admission application, register a student, evaluate transfer credits, image documents, etc. You don't necessarily need to be the fastest or the best at the task, but you do need to understand what it takes to do the work in your area. If you don't know these details, you can be "held hostage" by your staff or by other managers.

Hostages are at the mercy of others. Is the volume of work really so overwhelming that it cannot get done without additional help? Or is the process so cumbersome that what should take three minutes takes ten minutes? If you don't understand how your office functions, you will have to rely on what your staff tells you. At a meeting, another manager may surprise you by making a convincing case for moving some of his office's current functions into your area. Can you respond immediately and convincingly either for or against the proposal? If you understand your area, you have a good chance of knowing whether this would help your area or be overly burdensome. If you don't really know the details of how your office works, you likely will reply with the default statements "already overworked" or "I'll get back to you"—responses that may not be your best options.

KNOW WHEN TO QUIT

Because I now supervise a number of new deans and directors, I am giving a lot of thought to what type of advice I should be giving them. So I am certain that the epiphanies will keep coming. But I also am certain that you are busy and don't have time to read articles that ramble on. So I'll stop here and hope that these four epiphanies will serve you well!

8

CHAPTER EIGHT

Leadership by Respect

WILLIAM R. HAID

One of the

best things about getting older is that people sometimes think you must be smart or wise to have reached this point in your life. Even my kids now seem to think I may know a thing or two. As your hair turns gray, your wisdom or advice is more often sought, especially if you hold positions of leadership in your profession or in your community.

This phenomenon struck me most vividly when, at a recent meeting, a young professional said, "I'd like to get your opinion of a situation because I've heard that you are experienced in these matters." I'd just met this person, but either my reputation (which is what I'd like to think) or my graying hair (just as likely) caused her to consider me wise (or perhaps she was just being polite to a senior citizen!).

I started thinking about whether I could articulate a leadership style or philosophy that I have developed over the course of my career. Until now, I haven't tried to put a label on it, but I have shared my ideas with my colleagues, co-workers, and the handful of people I have been fortunate enough to mentor.

I call my philosophy "leadership by respect." And while I don't think I've ever heard of a leadership style by this name, I doubt it is original. My leadership style is driven by my core values: dignity, individual worth, and the belief that everyone is inherently equal to everyone else. Early in my career, I identified with a Bible verse that I subsequently adopted as my life statement: Romans 14:19 (ASV) says, "So then let us follow after things which make for peace, and things whereby we may edify one another." I am a peace maker. And I believe in building up others so they can become the best they can be, in work, in service, and in relationships.

How does leadership by respect work in the workplace? For me, it works quite well! How is it done? The following principles and practices equipped me to serve and lead at several successful organizations:

- Treat people respectfully. Learn their names, and use their names often and always. Protect the dignity of each person to others and to the individual. Never demean or joke about another person. Always give the benefit of the doubt and assume good intentions; allow the person the opportunity to prove otherwise before formulating a negative evaluation. Expect the best.
- Listen to others, and consider all opinions valid. Unless you know everything already, depend on others for expert opinion, and invite them to contribute to decisions.
- Value the contributions of everyone! No matter what each person's role in an organization, that role is important to the success of the organization.
- Give credit for success to others. Every organizational success is achieved as a result of the work of many. Rarely is anything accomplished by a single individual. Acknowledge achievements often, and celebrate successes regularly.

- Take responsibility for organizational failures. Every failure is an opportunity to learn and improve. Let those involved in any failures be part of a successful recovery. Don't punish unless the failures are intentional and repetitive.
- Share almost everything with everyone. Although some personnel, budget, and executive decisions are kept confidential until an appointed time, most other routine management information can be shared. The more people know about the hows and whys of their work environment, the more secure they feel in working toward organizational goals.
- Tell staff in your organization what your goals and plans are and why they are important. Share your plans with others, and they will adopt your plans as theirs.
- Give people the tools and permission to do their jobs. Update and upgrade office furnishings and technology when the opportunity presents itself. Reward staff with non-tangibles, such as office get-togethers, impromptu recognitions, removal of bureaucratic obstacles (when possible), support of their decisions with clients, and permitting them to make exceptions (within guidelines) to certain policies, practices, or procedures.

I have lived by these principles and have used them all in my work and volunteer activities. During my year as AACRAO president, a primary task was to incorporate the organization. The task included legal filings of articles of incorporation and modifying association bylaws to conform with the new articles. In some settings, these tasks might have been managed by a lawyer and/or staff members; but AACRAO is a membership-governed association, so the bylaws could be changed only by a vote by the membership.

I approached the task by appointing a task force of AACRAO members, officers, and staff. I selected people who cared deeply about the organization. There was no consensus about the outcome of this task; indeed, the task force members held highly divergent views of AACRAO. We began with a clear statement of why it was necessary to incorporate, and we considered the implications of incorporating as well as the risks of not incorporating. We detailed how this would be presented to the membership for approval, and we projected a timeline for doing so. I then asked each member to state his or her views on the task as well as any personal objectives in serving on the task force.

I proposed a process that would divide the task among work groups: Several members would develop a proposal for change of the bylaws or articles. The workgroups would present recommendations to the entire task force for final approval. I proposed that we require unanimity before including anything in the proposal to the members. The task force members agreed that we would operate in accordance with those principles.

The result was that we had an effective, efficient, and harmonious process for working through some complex governance structure issues. The next steps included communication with the membership and a vote during the annual business meeting. The proposal was accepted, and AACRAO was incorporated soon thereafter. Credit for this accomplishment is due to the task force members, who worked tirelessly to negotiate compromises and build consensus for the good of the association. Everyone won!

When I started my most recent job, at UC San Diego, I was advised that staff morale was low and that staff had been through more leadership change in recent years than their peers at most organizations. I wanted my staff to know that I would be a different leader for them—that I would be their advocate. I had met most of them once or twice during the interview and during my first few days on the job. At the first all-staff meeting, held during my first week on the job, I started by calling every one of the 22 staff members by name. This was not a big deal, but it constituted a good start to establishing a culture of leadership that knows and cares about each individual.

After three and a half years, the result is an organization that is moving in a positive direction. Survey results show high levels of employee satisfaction with leadership and in general. No, we have not had raises, and yes, we have had budget cuts. We've also focused on creating and maintaining a healthy organization, and we've had significant success with improving services to students and faculty. We are valued partners within our division and with the academic units we serve.

I have obtained similar positive results in every organization and at every institution where I have worked. That doesn't mean that I haven't made mistakes or that I haven't been unsuccessful in some individual cases. Some people cannot be led with respect and in fact don't respond well to any authority, organizational structure, or leadership. That said, I've been fortunate to witness some changes of heart by people who initially were distrustful.

I have seen some managers either flame out or leave a trail of destruction and hard feelings as a result of their basic rudeness and self-aggrandizement, self-centeredness, or lack of effort. That doesn't mean that organizational goals weren't obtained. But the results may have proven difficult to obtain, and the cost of such leadership is inevitably high in human terms.

My guess is that most managers use a combination of styles and philosophies that range from supportive to directive and that they value teamwork. Most managers want their organizations to be good places at which to work. Certainly, that has always been one of my goals.

A leader who starts with a culture and philosophy of respect can achieve much if he can provide a vision for the future and obtainable goals. One of my early mentors told me that if you want your employees to take good care of your customers, then you need to take good care of your employees. It's not that hard to do. Start with respect, and be consistent in your application of basic human kindness. You don't have to swim with sharks or be the last one standing to come out a winner.

9

CHAPTER NINE

Reflections on the Essentials of Leadership

CHRISTINE KERLIN

Chapter Nine

Two philosophers

on leadership have had great influence on me: Warren Bennis and John W. Gardner. I cannot speak or write about leadership without referring to one or both of them. I regard their perspectives as timeless.

Yes, I have also adopted the mantras of Kouzes and Posner, Max DuPree, and Robert K. Greenleaf, and I have paid attention to Covey's seven habits. And I would hope that you would consider their propositions as well, because they are solid and provide positive direction. But I will use this opportunity to discuss my interpretation of Bennis's (1996) "guiding vision, passion, and integrity" and Gardner's (1961) "excellence" perspectives because they are essential ingredients for those who are regarded as leaders—or who wish to act as leaders—in higher education and elsewhere. These perspectives illustrate how leaders can plant and cultivate the seeds of success in an organization or society, doing more than what is necessary simply to keep the farm's machinery running (though, of course, we value those people who keep the machinery running).

GUIDING VISION

Do you have a clear idea of what you want to do, and do you have the strength to persist? Your vision may include how your milieu is organized, how it functions, its goals, and its culture. You have looked beyond the immediate horizon and have envisioned "the best." This vision is the result of your own education and experience, your values, and consultation with others.

Most of us have several visions that guide us. We live in a complicated world where the ability to adjust, change, and transform is critical. We also have many divergent enterprises, such that a single vision just won't do. We have personal, community, and professional lives that call for different responses. That said, I believe that having a larger sense of how things should be—and the stamina to work toward its attainment—defines a leader.

How do these visions manifest themselves? On the individual level, we have seen colleagues lead committees, become executives, serve on boards, author chapters of books, and give conference presentations. In our organizations, we have seen examples of guiding visions: re-defining admission processes to recognize diverse learners; incorporating innovative technology for instructional and administrative purposes; internationalizing campuses; and, in AACRAO's case, in particular, advocating for public policy that is favorable to higher education and its constituents. On a larger scale, we have seen such examples of guiding visions as the GI Bill, the community college movement, and the Fulbright program. All of these—and more have required leadership and the strength to move beyond the status quo.

PASSION

We need to love what we are doing. That may be difficult to do every minute of the day, but we need to have an overriding passion for the promise of what we are doing.

Passion is linked to our guiding vision. It fires us up to carry through with our vision and our course of action. Passion also enables us to articulate our vision and build hope and inspiration in other people. Passion is contagious; used well, it encourages other people to buy in and strengthens their sense of purpose. This can put energy into a meeting, into a day, into a project—even into those times when things otherwise seem either a bit dry or terribly overwhelming.

In eleventh grade, my class was required to read *Man's Search for Meaning* by Viktor Frankl. There are many lessons one can choose to internalize from this book, but the lesson I have returned to over and over again is that we need to find what we love and hold on to its expectations of us; doing so provides the meaning and fulfillment that sustain what we need or want to do. This is, in short, the passion that energizes us.

Leaders work within systems, such as enrollment services offices, where some people may not occupy positions of any particular power and where their work may be tiring, routine, or monetarily unrewarding (or all three). Where is the passion there? I have found it particularly important to communicate the vision and the meaning (*i.e.*, the passion) of the work to such individuals and to recognize the ways in which their work has meaning and impact (often more than my own!). Kouzes and Posner (1990) offer insightful and relevant examples with their principles of "Model the Way," "Inspire a Shared Vision," "Enable Others to Act," and "Encourage the Heart."

INTEGRITY

We often refer to people we respect as having integrity. What is that intangible characteristic? Bennis (1994) identifies three essential aspects of integrity: self-knowledge, candor, and maturity.

Self-knowledge: How well do you know yourself—your strengths, your weaknesses? Do you vanquish the lies you could easily tell yourself? Do you identify your flaws and your assets and deal with them?

Candor: As the key to self-knowledge, are you honest with yourself? Have you identified the principles upon which you stand, and do you acknowledge them? Are you honest in your communications and actions?

Maturity: Are you able to locate within your own experience of being a follower the qualities of dedication, observation, teamwork, and honesty? Do you recognize those qualities and observe them in others? Have you learned from your errors?

I would add one further aspect of integrity: *conscience*, an inward sense of right and wrong. Stephen Covey (2002) notes that conscience is the one quality that is the difference between "leadership that works" and "leadership that endures." We can ascribe such values as fairness, respect, and contribution to the person with a conscience.

These personal characteristics enable the leader who possesses them to be a whole person—one with the capacity to develop a compelling and viable vision, to communicate an honest passion, to do the right thing, and to earn others' trust.

Many of us have worked with individuals who have been appointed leaders but who are neither honest nor fair, who have not faced their flaws, and whose experiences have not matured their perspectives. We don't respect or trust them. Such experiences in themselves should inform us of how we can strengthen our own integrity.

As leaders with integrity, we can point to the director who realizes that one of her shortcomings may be a poor understanding of the emerging technologies needed to achieve a vision or goal; who does not pretend that she does; who locates and acknowledges those who do possess that knowledge; and who engages openly with them on such issues. She demonstrates integrity even as she models how to empower others and direct their passion toward a vision.

EXCELLENCE

One aspect of excellence to link to the essential ingredients of leadership is the ability to recognize and extoll excellence in its many forms. Key to the success of an enterprise is the leader's recognition of the contributions that many make and that excellence comes from many quarters. No activity or action is too lowly to be regarded as valuable; neither does any high position ensure excellence simply because of its rank. Gardner's (1961) oft-quoted view is this: "The society which scorns excellence in plumbing as a humble activity and tolerates shoddiness in philosophy because it is an exalted activity will have neither good plumbing nor good philosophy: neither its pipes nor its theories will hold water."

The virtue of striving for excellence as we seek to achieve our mission goes almost without saying. Nevertheless, leaders, in emphasizing and recognizing excellence and value in their diverse forms and sources, can address those disquieting issues that arise when there are hierarchies—or even simply false distinctions—between leaders and followers. All of the people on our teams should be aware of their value and should be expected to produce excellent results; after all, it *all* has meaning, and it all matters.

CONCLUSION

The power of these essential ingredients produces a leader who becomes a servant. In the end, this is truly the role of the leader. The leader is attuned to the knowledge that she alone cannot achieve a vision or be the only one with passion. By recognizing the excellence and value present within the enterprise, the leader builds and shares vision and models and fuels passion. As a result of her self-knowledge, candor, and personal maturity, the leader inspires the trust of her colleagues to accept her service in the interest of moving forward *together*. Empowerment is shared.

I do not intend that the brevity of this essay should imply that leadership is simple and easy. Rather, leadership is a continual work in progress, and it certainly springs from more "ingredients" than those described here. Further, leadership is situational. We slip in and among roles of leader, follower, manager, and team member. Each role has its challenges and requisite skills.

These, however, are the essential points that inspire me. They have proven relevant to the situations I have endured. Whether I have lived up to the mark of leader is something for which my colleagues would have to vouch. I only know that it is a daily—if not hourly—challenge.

10

CHAPTER TEN

Making a Difference

GARY L. KRAMER

When it comes

to giving advice, I agree with colleagues who have stated that although we might give advice to aspiring professionals, it would be better yet if we would write or apply it to ourselves! So within that context, I, like my colleagues, do not claim to possess superior wisdom in student services. Rather, I claim that I have simply "toiled strenuously, conscientiously, and long enough to partially qualify as experienced in the field." (Please read James Appleton *et al.*, "Pieces of Eight…" for further insights from those who have toiled as leaders in student services.) My work has matured through the influence of those who have taught me to reach higher and surer in service and to keep perspective. Otherwise, I would not be writing this article.

I summarize my experience and advice in the following paragraphs. Certainly, there is no universal solution. What works for one may not necessarily work for another. But based on the aggregate of experience that resulted in the general guidelines provided below, individuals can adapt. Often, the best we can do is to decide on the best principle(s) of practice and move forward to integrate them into our personal style of management and personality until we gain confidence in and success with our work. When we are focused on student development and success, we cannot go too far amiss. After all, there is so much good work to be done that it is almost impossible for us to fail completely!

A BELLWETHER

Early in my career, Sara Looney, of George Mason University, introduced me to the notion of *bellwether*. I've tried to embrace it in my work ever since. I hope that you, too, will find it valuable as we consider "Making a Difference: Lessons Learned, Advice Given."

The term *bellwether* comes from the traditional practice of placing a bell around the neck of the sheep that leads the herd, thereby making it easier for others to follow. Now the word typically is applied in terms of leadership, as *influencing others to follow worthwhile standards and trends.* In today's vernacular, it is "making a difference" or focusing on "what matters most." Applying this definition, I would venture to say that making a difference in the field of student services is all about fostering a culture of success for students; in my view, this leads to personal and professional development and to campus-wide success.

BELLWETHER QUALITIES

Whether we seek to foster student success in the campus community or to find success in our professional endeavors, I have identified five characteristics of *bellwethers* that I believe are integral to making a difference in student services. The personal lessons I've learned and the advice I have to give are framed by "the five Cs" of bellwethers. Bellwethers are:

- committed;
- caring;
- collaborators;
- completers; and
- change makers.

I've also framed these bellwether characteristics around the following questions, which may prove helpful as we seek to make a difference and find success in our work:

- As you seek to move beyond the routine or expect to actually create and achieve a student-centered environment or culture of student success, what good models have been identified to emulate for both personal and program practices?
- What are the core characteristics found in successful individuals as well as in the programs they administer?
- What does research suggest as the next steps to consider and focus on to promote student success and development, *e.g.*, what do student services providers need to do better in order to align expectations, connect services, actively foster student development, and consistently achieve results through student-oriented services and programs?

Bellwethers are committed to student success and development.

First, bellwethers are committed to students' development and success. They seek to revitalize the academic community by maintaining a process of constructive response to new needs. They focus on what is working and what is not—questions that have been and always will be a primary focus of successful administrators.

Although they may find it challenging to do so, bellwethers must put students first as partners in the learning enterprise. They must recognize that students' success and their own success are directly aligned—like collaborative partnerships. Student services professionals must always consider how to more effectively engage students in examining the alignment of their expectations and experiences with the claims of the institution. Only then can we go and do what William Butler Yeats described in this challenge: "Education is not the filling of a pail but the lighting of a fire of learning."

Bellwethers care.

A good friend of mine, John Gardner, asked an assembly of faculty and administrators to reflect on who in their educational journey made a difference or served as a positive role model. Similarly, I ask, whom will our students remember long after their college experience is over? Whom will they remember as having made a difference in their lives, as having put them first, and as having enabled and ennobled them to achieve success?

Who helped you make the connection between your personal and academic lives? What was the defining moment for you? My guess is that this person cared about you. Long after you forgot the information and advice the individual gave, you likely remember the gift of self—perhaps the most detectable and memorable part of our professional work.

Bellwethers collaborate.

Bellwethers foster the success and dignity of each person in the campus community. Truly, it takes a campus to raise a successful student. I believe in teamwork. Coordination and collaboration are essential, especially when organizational lines are flattened in order to achieve the most important goal: student success. (What objective must a campus community undertake immediately upon students' admission other than to contribute unceasingly to their success in attaining their academic goals?) To "flatten" academic resources through campus collaboration is to enable students and others to contribute to the effective management and wise use of student services. To be successful, we must focus on shared responsibilities and partnerships. We can learn from one another, especially when we consolidate our services in support of student success.

Educational demographer Harold Hodgkinson observed that the key to promoting student success on campus is to know the students who are entering and to monitor their progress. Constant effort is required to adjust and balance student services—to include providing purposeful direction and placing students on a more successful track when services are not working well.

Bellwethers are completers.

Bellwethers are initiators and innovators more than responders and imitators. They complete what they set out to do because they methodically develop—in concert with others—a plan or strategy to improve services; in addition, they participate integrally in executing the plan. Bellwethers also recognize that funds for new programs almost always come from old programs; few receive new money.

Bellwethers believe (as Will Rogers did) that even those who are on the right track will get run over if they just sit there. Accordingly, bellwethers are purposeful in their work, *i.e.*, aligning institutional claims consistently and persistently to determine how current services are and what is of most value to students and the campus. Bellwethers are completers because they consistently and persistently engage stakeholders—including faculty, staff, students, and campus leadership—in focusing and integrating student services that meet the claims or expectations of the institution.

Bellwethers are change agents.

Bellwethers view themselves as more than managers of services and controllers of behavior. Rather, they are policy strategists who use a set of administrative principles as well as technology and data to make informed decisions. They actively incorporate their own confidence, competence, and integrity as well as that of their colleagues.

Knowing he was terminally ill, Randy Pausch, a computer science professor at Carnegie Mellon University, wrote *The Last Lecture*, encouraging others to overcome obstacles and seize the moment to do what matters most. Essentially and reflectively, Pausch asked his audiences, "If we were to vanish tomorrow, what would we want as our legacy?" Similarly, he asked what we would want our narrative to be five years from now. What creative energy and ambition would we need to summon now to initiate progress for improvement—in our case, to make a difference in our work as student services leaders? In the end, what will *our* narrative as bellwethers be?

CONCLUSION

If I were asked to provide a baker's dozen of lessons learned and advice given on the basis of more than four decades in higher education, it would be something like this:

- Be loyal to your institution. *Not everything that counts can be counted, and not everything that can be counted counts,* but loyalty will always be counted.
- Remember that good teachers/mentors are scholars, and good scholars are good teachers/mentors. Wisely and productively use research and data to inform decision making.
- Foster student development and success while emphasizing and empowering through shared responsibility. "Translate ideas into events to serve people," said Thor Heyerdahl.
- Do not take yourself too seriously. Take your job seriously, but not yourself. Smile more often. You'll receive praise, honor, and criticism—probably simultaneously. So learn and don't inhale—at least not deeply. Robert Frost said, "A truly educated person is one who can listen to anything and not lose his temper or his self-confidence."
- Be positive and celebrate successes—both others' achievements and your own accomplishments. Most situations have positive and negative sides. I advise that you take the high road whenever possible. That is, don't get caught up in the thick of thin things!
- Develop a work ethic that leads you to exceed expectations. Be passionate about your work and be open to learning something worthwhile each day even from your mistakes. Mark Twain said,

"Good judgment comes from experience, and where does experience come from? Experience comes from bad judgment."

- Recognize and acknowledge diverse learners on campus, and seek to serve a broad range of values and viewpoints; understand the diversity on your campus, and particularly the unique needs of the diverse learners you serve.
- Remember that influence should develop from integrity, honesty, and competency in all matters, great and small. Influence relates to quality of performance, quality of values, the quality of behavior, and the quality of one's treatment and response to others and their needs. *Only the mediocre are at their best all the time.*

  BYU Educator Karl Maeser provided this insight and good advice on integrity and honor:

  > *Place me behind prison walls—walls of stone ever so high, ever so thick, reaching ever so far into the ground—there is the possibility that in some way or another I will escape. But stand me on the floor and draw a chalk line around me and have me give my word of honor never to cross it. Can I get out of the circle? No. Never! I'd die first.*

- Don't forget to dream. And while you dream, remember that the true calling of higher education is to create a community that includes the success and dignity of each individual on campus.
- "Flow" (*i.e.*, the optimal experience or success) is something we make happen. But remember: When you teach a bear to dance, be prepared to dance until the bear wants to stop.
- Engage others in decision making so that all "own" the decision.
- Maximize the power of creative tension: Recognize and be prepared to work with a generative and adaptive learning community.
- Build a culture of evidence of success. Assessments that really matter (*i.e.*, that are purposeful) align the institution with its claims for achieving personal and institutional outcomes. Be-

cause we value what we measure, institutions and personnel should focus assessment and accountability efforts on what matters to student success.

Individuals who work in student services can make a difference—in fact, a collective positive difference—to their own success as well as to that of students by consistently doing things that matter most. What we do for others—especially students—is returned to us. Student learning, growth, and success are the responsibility of everyone on campus. If we incorporate the "five Cs of bellwethers" into our individual work in student services, we ultimately can foster a culture of success for everyone in the campus community. Ultimately, each of us must determine our own success indicators as well as our objectives for those we serve, all within the context of our resources and time. Each of us must decide what matters most in fostering student success on campus and making a difference. But perhaps the most important question to be addressed is what our "narrative" as student services professionals will be. John Wesley summed up our work in these words:

Do all the good you can,
By all the means you can,
In all the ways you can,
At all the times you can,
To all the people you can,
As long as you can.

As you chart your personal and professional narrative, I hope that the lessons learned and the advice I have given will prove helpful.

11

CHAPTER ELEVEN

Lessons Learned from a Life in Theatre

SUSAN LEIGH

Although flattering,

it feels somewhat ironic to me that I should give advice to new AACRAO professionals. As I remember it, it was only yesterday when I myself was seeking such advice from seasoned colleagues, trying to find my way, trying to define my role as a newcomer in student records administration. You see, for the first 20 years of my professional university life, I was an academic: theatre performance was at the core of all I did as a professor. During that period, I never anticipated that my professional path would lead to academic administration. From being on stage as a teenager in community theatre, to my BA in theatre, to professional equity performing, and then to graduate school for an MFA in acting followed by certification to coach actors in speech for the stage, I had more than 100 production credits before I transitioned into administration. I balanced my work life and my private life between the worlds of professional and academic theater. I moved fluidly between teaching in university conservatories across the country and working in professional theatres. I felt completely fulfilled and blessed because I was able to do everything I loved: teach, direct, coach, and perform. When I accepted a position to teach acting and speech in the Theatre School at DePaul University, I was beyond energized. I started a small "off-loop" theatre in my spare time, earned tenure in three years, and engaged myself in the cultural worlds of Chicago and the Theatre School.

But it was the larger institutional culture of DePaul University that actually turned my head—that got me interested in administration. If you are a professor who is passionate about teaching, as I was, you quickly realize that with hard work, you can have an impact on the lives of your students. And that is powerful and fulfilling! But if you are an administrator who is passionate about student success, you can have an impact on the lives of *thousands* of students currently enrolled at your institution as well as on new students and alumni. And that can be even more powerful, even more fulfilling! I feel privileged to work in central administration, where I bring my classroom perspective and have the chance to impact so many students as part of my job.

With its strong mission and Vincentian values in which everyone seems to believe, DePaul has an almost palpable—and addictive—ethos. I quickly sought ways to be engaged in the community in any way I could. Faculty committees, research and grants, task forces... this high-level engagement is the match that we talk about in enrollment management when we tell students they will find success when they find the school that best fits them personally. We tell students that they will know when it happens; in like manner, I felt the systemic pull of engagement and belonging to DePaul's academic community. For the first time, I wanted to learn all I could about how universities worked—and even more about why *this* university was so different. The more I learned, the more I cared and committed; to date, my relationship with DePaul has lasted 20 years. Coming here was the best thing I ever did in the course of my career.

So exactly what are secrets to success? I am sure I do not know. Nevertheless, I can tell you what lessons I have learned as an academic—and a theatre person, at that—who came to administration with seemingly different skills and experiences from "the usual." The greatest lesson is that *you bring something unique to the table,* so don't change or adapt in order to be like everyone else. I brought many skills and lessons learned as an artist that one might think totally inapplicable, but I learned that one's uniqueness, above all, is one's personal strength, and it will fuel your personal contributions. Don't be sure that you know all that you have to offer; after all, the best working environment—the one that is your "match"—will draw out things you have learned elsewhere.

FIND YOUR MATCH! MATCH YOUR PASSION!

I apologize for sounding Pollyanna-ish, but I can attest to the fact that if you truly love where you work, you will flourish in your career while you are there. If you are in a place that matches your energy and where you work to achieve a shared vision with people you admire, you will relax, feel supported, become your best self, and work from inner strengths that are not accessible to you in environments where you feel you do not fit in, where you cannot relate to others. A critical part of all retention strategies is to make every effort to help new students feel they belong—that they are part of the fabric of the institution—as soon as possible after they arrive. We urge our first-year students to become engaged in the community of learners on campus because that engagement will inspire their academic success. As professionals, we should make the same demands of ourselves; after all, the time and energy we invest in our institution is a deposit against which we can later draw as we build our career. Leadership positions and promotions come because you make a commitment, take advantage of opportunities to learn more about the institution, and, inadvertently, learn about yourself. Energy and engagement make you "present" in the room and attract similar energy, making you stand out.

BE CREATIVE

Leaders envision a future and then take others there, negotiating and brokering step by step along the way, building trust even through thick fog, leading the group because they really do know the way, because they can envision the end result. When I was directing, theatres would give me a script and ask me to stage it in their season. I never would direct a play that did not generate pictures upon my first read. If I could envision the world of the play, then I could lead the cast, crew, and designers toward that vision. And with powerful team dynamics on my side, I could create the world of the play. It is the same in leadership roles within the academy: I must be able to see a way to accomplish the end, to define the success of projects, new initiatives, implementations, strategic planning, etc. Be creative in your visions, and find new solutions to old issues. And if you can help others see what success looks like, they will help you achieve it (they may even help get you the funding!).

PLANNING

Project planning has become an important part of the administrator's role because of regular systemic implementations, among other things. Know how many staff take how many hours to get the job done now; how staff time on task will decrease once you implement the new solution; and how you will reallocate their time. With old-fashioned observation and math, you can build a case and then provide proof of concept. I know how many hours I need to rehearse a play with a cast before opening a show. And I have found dependable ways of measuring time on task in student records processing so that we know what and when we can deliver on a project, even in the midst of all the other things we do. Always have contingency plans for everything you do, because you never know...you could be wrong. Keep that new plan to yourself, but be ready to implement it quickly should you discover that you cannot do what you promised. You see, more and more, the new directions we take in academic administration involve collaboration across and among offices, and sometimes their resources and enthusiasm for a project may fail to match yours.

NEGOTIATING AND BROKERING

Theatre is a collaborative art which cannot happen with one lone artist. Even one-person shows have a crew behind the scenes that makes things happen, even if it never appears on stage. I learned early how to focus on shared objectives in rehearsal and production while finding my own unique individual way to contribute to the whole. This kind of collaborative experience clearly has shaped me, because even in my current work, I look for that obligation to partner that is inherent in theatre as an art form. Others may not have had comparable experiences where the end product belongs to so many—where it rests on the success of so many individual pieces and you have to be patient. A symphony of small decisions, any major project requires the buy-in of all those who will be affected by its outcome. You have to use high-level negotiating and brokering skills to help others see the benefits, to persuade others to support your vision. It is never easy to convince naysayers, so don't let others tell you that it is; that said, few other things will give you such a strong sense of accomplishment.

CHANGE

Plan for it, embrace it, get out in front of it, or change will control you! Early in my career, I had the opportunity to work on many new plays. A new script develops right in front of you once you put the script in actors' hands, but hours of rehearsal can pass before the real direction and shape of the work are revealed. Eventually, everyone in the room knows if a particular scene is working or if it needs to be rewritten or even cut, perhaps because it is pulling the entire story line off track. Peter Senge has written so much about change and opportunities for change, in particular. He tells us that innovation is not problem solving; rather, it is learning how to do something new. Problem solving merely "fixes" the thing that you have. Whether you are talking about staff hours, implementation budget dollars, time within the academic calendar, or virtually anything else, you have only so many resources. So if you continue to add things that necessarily will require a portion of those finite resources, then you will need to let go of a process or procedure that you do now. Senge suggests that administrators implement a regular "search and destroy" process—that is, regularly look for things to leave behind in order to make room for the new things. For example, in my office, staff are prompted to regularly question and reflect on what they do. Which processes—in whole or in part—don't make sense anymore? What might be a better way? Trust those individuals who perform the processes because they really do know when something should be changed. And remember that while the tools change all the time, the values stay the same.

TELL THE STORY

Know your material; learn your lines! "Script" yourself to ensure that you have chosen the most impactful language, and practice until those words belong to you—until you are comfortable speaking them. You must be able to make your points—to tell the story—clearly and succinctly. Use data and not emotion to describe the circumstances, and then allow your listeners to arrive at your conclusion, where you will be waiting patiently for them. The right data used at the right moment will position you and your idea for a timely decision. They will ensure that you will be successful in garnering support—financial as well as ideological.

Tell the story of success by providing data; justify the investment in the project, and demonstrate that you improved the service just as you said you would. If you have to submit a report, be concise. Learn the value of the one-page summary (sometimes that's all that decision makers have time to read). Years ago, when I was quite new to executive reporting, I felt insulted when, having spent hours writing a long and detailed project report, I was asked by the EVP to distill it to one page. In response, I created a template; I noted when it was successful, and I changed it when it was not. Learn to write a one-pager that accurately explains your project without jargon or emotion and that outlines in the most objective way what you need the leadership to know (or, better yet, what you need them to do). Be sure their action items immediately follow the conclusions!

LIFELONG LEARNING: RESEARCH, READ, AND REFLECT

Research: Be curious! Learn from colleagues on your own campus as well as on others. Pick up the phone, introduce yourself, and ask that question—or invite her to lunch or for a drink. Even though our institutions compete for students, you soon will find that there are professional relationships to be made that will prove extremely valuable. Reach out, and get to know the competition.

Be ready to learn. To succeed in today's academic environment, you need to develop multiple literacies. Doubtless, you will find new ways to solve old problems, to research new systemic solutions, to adapt them for your institutional culture, and to implement them quickly and efficiently. This kind of research and development demonstrates that you are willing to jump in, acquire new skills and competencies, and test your native abilities in ways you have never imagined. You cannot develop realistic expectations for staff members' use of new technologies if you yourself are unfamiliar with those technologies, so get in there and learn as much as you can.

Make time to read! Look outward. Take time every week to read about academia from a national perspective. What are the best practices nationwide for your area of administration? What are other schools doing that you might replicate on your campus? Can you imagine what take-away might be yours if you were to bring a team for a site visit? (How often do we look to each other for a solution when the best ideas may be within reach but at another institution?) In my experience, colleagues were generous—more than willing to share their successes and challenges; I have tried to adopt the same code of conduct. It is profoundly rewarding to receive help from a colleague; and almost all are willing and able to help.

Reflect: After a project concludes, an especially busy season subsides, or a long and difficult implementation ends, take time with your team to look back and assess what worked well and why as well as what didn't work and why. Schedule retreats, moratorium meetings, and brainstorming sessions, and draft assessment reports. Plan to combine the team's intellectual capital in productive ways to determine together how you can "work smarter."

REVIEWS

Listen and learn from all your critics, whether friend or foe. (Sometimes your enemies more clearly reveal where you should focus your attention next.) Accept all constructive criticism, and be grateful: You will get better if you are willing to listen. Beware faint praise as it will never help you become a better professional. Be grateful for the standing ovations and raves when they come, but stay focused on student success—not politics—as the critical milestone.

One famous director counted how many patrons left the theatre at intermission; believing them to be too challenged by his work, he claimed their departure to be his success. Retention and graduation rates are our goals in higher education administration, but not at all costs. We want students to be happy with their experiences inside and outside the classroom, so be willing to listen to suggestions of how your area might serve students better. After all, students can vote with their feet and may choose to enroll elsewhere. And unlike my artistic friend, we want them to stay for the second act!

TAKE SOME RISKS!

Yes, academic leaders must know certain rules and regulations and ensure institutional compliance, but they also must learn how to think through an exception. Where does compliance end and the spirit of the law begin? Be sure to contextualize what the real impact is on the students involved as well as on the institution. This is a critical judgment; you must know the culture of your institution to understand how risk averse it may be.

BALANCE LIFE AND WORK

To maintain the zest, enthusiasm, and boundless energy that you require in your position year after year, you must make sure that you can step away for some personal time every day, every week, and for an extended period or two every year; then you will return to work rested and refreshed. Hope, optimism, and future-mindedness are qualities that successful leaders must possess. If you remember to take time to recharge, you will have the positive energy necessary to lead. Above all, make sure that you have fun at work as well as in your personal life. In the theatre, when things get way too serious, we often remind each other that it is a "play," after all, and that we should find a way to make the work fun. "Ten-thirty always comes!" was the advice one famous playwright used to give when things onstage were most challenging. Similarly, in academia, this term will end, you will get through it together as a team, and you will get a chance to do better the next time. And we always do! Don't keep looking back. Instead, anticipate all the good things that are about to come. Keep the vision alive!

12

CHAPTER TWELVE

Observations from Climbing the Leadership Ladder

PAUL P. MARTHERS

Chapter Twelve

The first time

I became "the boss" I was sixteen and working at a cheese factory in Vermont. One afternoon the second shift foreman took me aside and said, "I'm putting you in charge of making block cheddar." There was no more explanation. The foreman was a man of few words, but enough to tell two guys who were older than me that I was now their project supervisor. So for the next month, I lead the process of mixing and raking, draining and cutting, gathering and scooping, and then dumping thumb-size, rubbery chunks of cheddar into tins that got pressed with a hydraulic arm. Like many first bosses, I had no training. Nobody gave me a manual for leadership in cheese making. Even so, the men I led listened to me, the work got done, and the quality of the cheddar won praise from a factory owner whose infrequent appearances on the production floor always sent shivers of terror through the cheese crew.

That summer experience and the college application essays it inspired set me on the path to where now, as vice president for enrollment at a 7,500-student technological university, I lead the divisions of undergraduate admissions, financial aid, graduate admissions, and enrollment operations. As a member of the president's cabinet, much of the leadership I exercise occurs through oversight and problem-solving committees comprised of trustees, deans, other vice presidents, or all of the above. My current position, when compared to past leadership posts, is more strategic leader than day-to-day manager. In director and deans positions (at Oberlin College and at Reed College), I managed departments. As a vice president, I manage the people who manage the departments. The latter is a different skill, one that leaders acquire only as they move up.

Between supervising the block cheddar project at age sixteen and becoming director of an admissions office, more than 20 years intervened. Counting the jobs I held through college, I toiled on the proverbial lower rungs of the ladder for more years than I have been "the boss." All those years working my way up the ladder were invaluable, arguably more valuable than a meteoric rise in my twenties to boss might have been, because while traveling the slower road (and enduring the accompanying frustrations) to the leader's chair, I learned a good deal about how leaders are viewed by the people they lead. Few of us ever get the ideal boss who takes us under wing and teaches us best leadership practices. As a result, there is utility in recognizing what can be learned from the unfortunately more common experience of working under people whose approaches will never appear in any handbook of best leadership practices.

Certainly it would be nice to have all the answers. But the best leaders know that is impossible. In fact great leaders tend to be very good at knowing what they do not know. I have seen the counterproductive effect of the opposite type of leader, the one who must be the smartest person in every room. Meetings conducted by leaders whose views must always be right and never open to challenge are like sitting in an echo chamber. From this type of leadership, subordinates learn that it is dangerous to think for oneself or to express divergent opinions. Leadership of this type turns subordinates into bobble heads who constantly nod yes and acquiesce to the leader's demands—even if they can see that their leader is steering the whole organization into a massive iceberg. Lead like this and not only will your employees stop telling you the truth, they will also be constantly looking to jump ship.

It is nearly impossible to lead a division or institution effectively and still act like the working director of its various departments. Although conscientious detail management is a skill prized in project managers, leaders of complex organizations need to step back and let their employees do the jobs they were hired to do. Truly effective leaders advance to ever higher positions because they are not controlling micromanagers who expect everyone under them to do things their way. The leader who cannot let go and insists on acting like the director of every department often misses the big strategic picture due to an unhealthy obsession with the minor details. Most of us have seen this type of leader crash up against the Peter Principle. I recall bosses with desks piled high with all the memos and letters that had to be read and edited en route to approval. In one of those cases, key communications did not go out, numerous program deadlines passed, and departmental output slowed noticeably--resulting in swift termination for the bottleneck-creating leader.

Knowing that your way is not the only way and recognizing that you have knowledge gaps that others can fill are sure signs of leadership self-confidence. Good leaders show this by hiring and promoting people with complementary skills, not simply those who are clones of themselves. They know that innovation occurs in environments where leaders cultivate creative and even divergent ways of thinking, not uniformity. Insistence on a unified front might work when managing a high profile crisis situation, but as a day to day leadership style it is stifling to the people you manage.

Managing by command and control techniques that cultivate fear of and obedience to the leader may work for football coaches or for military officers, but such approaches often prove disastrous in the shared governance environment of higher education. Authority founded on fear of the leader's power to punish sends many talented people in higher education heading for the exits, engenders shallow loyalty at best, and creates low morale work environments. Leaders who scare others into submission rather than inspiring them to reach for greatness should beware: when the oppressed subjects rise up en masse, the dictatorial leader will fall fast.

There is a big difference between being a friendly boss and being the boss as friend. The boss as friend tends to invite jealously (often unwittingly) as well as charges of playing favorites. Do not for a minute believe that everyone understands and accepts that you and employee X often go trout fishing after work simply because you share an interest in fly rods. In such cases, it will not be long before jealously reveals its ugly fangs and someone accuses the boss of being a closer friend to some (such as the fishing buddy) than to others. The boss as friend may also find that taking corrective action against an underperforming employee elicits a startled and hurt response such as, "but I thought we were friends." Before falling into the boss as friend trap, remember that the people you lead recognize that you are the boss. If they understand professionalism, they will not expect, nor will they want you, to be their friend. In fact, the expectation that they be the boss' friend is frequently viewed by employees as a burden. The kind of boss that the institution you serve, and the people you lead, need you to be is one who is firm, fair, and friendly. And the friendly part of firm, fair, and friendly does not mean friend.

Now isn't it obvious that no one in their right mind would want to practice the misguided approaches to leadership just described? One would think so. Unfortunately, just drawing from my own experiences working for nine institutions over the years, I have seen all of the above types of ineffective leadership approaches more than once. While I cannot write a cure-all prescription outlining exactly how to practice good leadership, I can say with conviction to any new leader, do not act like the bosses described above. Still, getting advice regarding best practices and observing examples of good leadership will only take new leaders so far. Practicing good leadership on the job is the true test.

In their daily roles, leaders are asked to make the final decision on many matters, even those outside their realm of expertise. Leadership requires making decisions that solve problems, and solving a problem requires understanding the situation from all sides (if that is possible) or at least using the best available information. Recognizing that others may know more about the situation than you do is a prerequisite for solving (rather than needlessly creating) problems. For this reason, good leaders need to temper the tendency toward broadcast mode—admittedly a mode that can inspire and persuade others—to listen actively to what is really going on at the institution. Listening results in the leader grasping the mood and culture of the institution—and solutions that factor in the mood and culture of the school are usually the most effective ones. Listening shows that the leader understands the significant place that the airing of diverse viewpoints has in educational institutions. Still, grasping the importance of participatory discussion and listening does not translate into leaders needing to operate according to direct-vote democracy. Turning every issue into a community referendum is an abdication of leadership and a sure route to eroding respect in the leader's authority while begging the question is a leader even necessary. People tend to want leaders to lead, and leading is not giving everybody what they want all the time.

Understandably, leaders approach their new job with ideas and eagerness to move their institution forward. But effective leaders also know to devote significant time in their early days to discovering how and why things operate in certain ways. One failsafe way to get off to a good start is for the leader to go on a listening tour of personal engagement around the community. A listening tour will signal that the leader approaches the new institution with the recognition that it is a distinctive entity with a particular character, culture, and set of attributes to be comprehended, clarified and then factored into any resulting strategic plan for progress. Through the process of eliciting perspectives from around the campus, the effective leader can begin to craft a vision for future accomplishment and build bonds on which consensus and collaboration can be founded.

My concluding lesson for leaders is a bit of a paradox. The best leaders, those who bring together people and resources to achieve progress and surmount hurdles, often do so in ways that make their leadership appear seamless (even invisible), creating an impression of "we did this" rather than "I did this." To leave their institution in a better place than they found it, the best leaders know that their efforts are truly successful only if progress continues uninterrupted even after the leader, who was the catalyst for the progress, departs.

13

CHAPTER THIRTEEN

The Three Fs of Leadership

BRYAN NEWTON

Everyone

should have the experience of working in higher education. The customs and traditions of academia, the diversity of backgrounds and experiences among faculty and staff, and the excitement that comes with the beginning of each new semester are truly unique. Sixteen-week blocks of time come and go in what seems like the blink of an eye. In the midst of preparing for semesters, closing out semesters, and trying to move initiatives forward in the sparse time between, it is easy to overlook what a privilege it is to be part of a campus community that helps students achieve their goals and fulfill their dreams.

I am grateful to have the opportunity to be a college leader. However, as I reflected upon what words of wisdom I might share for this leadership series, it occurred to me that not everyone shares my sense of gratitude. There are far too many days when higher education leaders get bogged down by the weight of responsibility and the day-to-day distractions that are part of college administration.

Of course, we shouldn't feel burdened or distracted because we are leaders (at least that's what the world wants us to believe). Walk into your local bookstore, find the leadership section, and glance at what is on the shelf: There are books detailing how great leaders became great, books with five- and ten-step plans to becoming great leaders, books to help teach the great leaders of the future, and dozens of other leadership texts that extol the virtues of leadership.

Both the popular and scholarly literature perpetuate this halo effect. Leaders are equated to heroes who rush in and save the day. The subtle message is that leadership is the answer to whatever ails an organization. Leaders have all the answers! And if you just hire the right one, everything will be fine.

Society suggests that we should search for leaders who are excellent (or, to quantify excellence in academic terms, leaders who would earn As in our classrooms), but perhaps we should help leaders to acquire a few Fs. To those currently in leadership positions—young leaders who are just beginning their careers in new roles—and to those who aspire to become leaders in higher education, I offer three Fs they should strive to attain: failure, followership, and flexibility.

FAILURE

One of my favorite movie scenes is from the 1987 film *Wall Street:* The hot shot stockbroker Bud Fox, played by Charlie Sheen, is moments away from being arrested for insider trading. Before this tragic fall from grace, an older, wiser colleague puts his arms around Bud and says, "Man looks into the abyss, and there's nothing staring back at him. At that moment, that's when a man finds his character, and that's what keeps him out of the abyss."

Leaders fail. I believe that we learn from failure not only how to perform tasks better, but also—and more important—about our character. Failure teaches us to acknowledge our humanity and to realize that perfection is a fool's errand and an expectation that we should not set for ourselves or those we lead. Rather, we should strive for excellence, improvement, and the satisfaction that comes with knowing we have given our best effort to the task at hand.

Likewise, failure helps to build the character that is vital when we experience loss or bend under the weight of great responsibility. Bending and not breaking is the result of having learned from failure. A leader in higher education faces any number of challenges on a daily basis. We want leaders who can face challenges with the fortitude required to rebound from momentary defeat.

Failure and how we handle it are vital to successful leadership. As a character from another movie once uttered, "Failure is not an option."

FOLLOWERSHIP

Enrollment management leaders play a pivotal role in attracting and retaining students for the institutions we serve. Like most leaders, we are credited with great success when things go well (*i.e.*, when enrollment increases) and blamed when things take a turn for the worse (*i.e.*, when enrollment decreases). Yet too often the successes and failures of organizations are evaluated solely on the basis of the perceived performance and abilities of a single person.

Think again of the bookstore I mentioned earlier. The leadership section likely includes many books about leadership but very few about followership. Leadership is observed, evaluated, and discussed according to a leader-centric rather than a follower-centric approach. While authors such as Barbara Kellerman and Jean Lipman-Blumen have begun to explore followership, the subject is still largely unexplored and ignored.

All leaders have had experiences as followers. Leaders should be mindful of their past and present roles as followers and should remember the concept of followership as they interact with those around them. To become a good leader, one must explore his own followership: Think about how you perceive and react to actions by leaders and the positive and negative results in the interactions in which you are a follower. Use these lessons to improve your relationships with followers and to gain a better understanding of how they perceive your communication and behavior. In addition, teach supervisors in your departments to consider followership.

To put it simply, stand in the shoes of those you lead, and consider how they perceive your leadership. Taking time on a regular basis to reflect on followership will help you become a better leader. After all, it is followers and their actions that are most likely to lead not only to your success but also to that of your institution.

FLEXIBILITY

Franklin D. Roosevelt is believed to have said that "rules are not necessarily sacred; principles are." During my tenure as a college administrator, many new hires from outside higher education have shared their difficulty in adjusting to an environment with so many policies, procedures, and regulations. At a public institution—a college or university system, in particular—the rules are even more complex.

Of course, we need rules, and it is imperative to spend time developing policy and procedures for our institutions. A good leader emphasizes the importance of adhering to the rules and of ensuring that we are ethical and transparent in all of our dealings. Institutional accreditors emphasize this as well, and we all are aware of the consequences to our institutions and students when policies and procedures either are disregarded or are nonexistent.

Nevertheless, leaders must take President Roosevelt's statement to heart and be open to the possibility of being flexible in their application of the rules. This is one of the differences between a manager and a leader: A manager is likely to enforce the rules to the letter whereas a leader should be willing at least to consider extenuating circumstances, the best interest of the student, the best interest of the institution, and other mitigating factors. I am not advocating that leaders break from policy and procedure without considered judgment. However, leaders must understand the value of flexibility and their greater duty to ensure that students and institutions are not harmed by blanket enforcement of the rules.

Flexibility has one other application as an "F word" for leaders, and that is in relation to the work environment we provide for our followers. Leaders should not make difficult the work of those they have been entrusted to lead. Unfortunately, I have seen too many so-called leaders make work and life unnecessarily difficult for their followers. I urge leaders to be flexible in their supervision and understanding of each individual's professional situation. Our goal as leaders should be to help develop our followers and to make every effort to create the best work environment for them that we can. To do otherwise is a breach of the trust that has been placed in us as leaders and is contrary to the essence of good leadership.

We should be willing to incorporate some other "F words" into our leadership practice: *Forgiveness,* though often recognized solely as a spiritual concept, is critical if we are to avoid revenge, anger, and other pitfalls of leadership. *Fortitude* is also necessary for any good leader to survive both the highs and the lows that come with the position. *Fidelity* should be another element of leadership as we honor our commitments as higher education leaders to students, faculty, staff, and the community.

My advice to leaders is to earn a few Fs: Be willing to fail; understand followership; and practice flexibility.

14

CHAPTER FOURTEEN

Creating a Culture of Success for Staff

LISA MOSELE SCULLY

After finishing

my undergraduate degree in English, my first employment was in an academic department at my alma mater. At a large public state institution, the salary scale for non-academic appointees was—and remains—woefully low. Knowing that monetary compensation wasn't the source of staff satisfaction, my chairman made a dedicated effort to create the best work environment possible within the constraints of university regulations.

Initially promising a two-year commitment, I ended up staying eleven years and earning a master's degree in higher education/ student affairs. In fact, for several years, each of us in the office—including the entry-level, front-line secretaries—held a master's degree. Why did I (and many of my colleagues) stay in the department so long? As I joined the Office of the Registrar and took on management of a much more numerous staff, I asked myself that question.

The answer was the culture in the office. I knew I wanted to create an environment like the one I had just left, where people enjoyed being in the office, even when the work wasn't always stimulating or fulfilling on its own merits. What did I need to bring to establish and then sustain that culture with this new group of people?

My answers aren't news to those who read management literature, but they have a proven track record of more than 25 years. Begin with a foundation of mutual respect; build confidence in the team through mutual trust; strengthen connections through open communication; and always maintain a sense of humor.

James Joyce said that "children must be educated by love, not punishment." Only when I became a parent myself did I realize how easily extensible Joyce's quote was to management. As I helped my son build his tool kit for navigating relationships, I realized that respect and trust such as I was shown by my mentor were as critical to my early growth as an administrator as they were to my son's development.

My ability to manage was a given for my chairman, and he empowered me to do so with confidence by providing a general sense of parameters as well as clearly communicated policies. I also was given a framework within which to make my decisions and was trusted to run the department of more than 100 faculty and instructors so the chairman could continue to focus on his own research needs. My chairman never met my decisions with frustration or recriminations. In turn, I established guidelines so that each staff member could succeed at her duties.

We knew that it was okay to make mistakes. Our chairman acknowledged our intelligence, trusted our judgment, and supported and guided us through mistakes as well as the murky waters of administrative minutiae. And we succeeded, without fear of reprisals or reprimands, because we knew it was safe to make mistakes—especially as we learned from them.

So my first lesson for successful management is to lead from your heart. Talk with your staff. An open door signals that an open mind governs the desk inside the office. Be there; be present for problems of all sizes and from all aspects of people's lives. Celebrate people's successes, both personal and professional, and allow time to grieve when sorrows strike. If you naturally think from the heart, it's okay to embrace that part of your personality. Note, however, that this does not necessarily mean to become best friends with each staff member. It's critical to maintain a professional relationship with those whom one manages. Just remember that 'professional' doesn't have to mean 'aloof.'

Second, whether or not it comes easily, it is critical that you communicate. Trust your staff to understand the challenging issues and to appreciate hearing the bad news from you, before rumors start. Provide your staff with as much detail as is prudent; this shows respect for their contributions and attests to their worth in your eyes.

Another favorite quote is from Frank Hohengarten, who said, "The purpose of management is to create an organization that doesn't need you." Thus, my third lesson is to define your policy boundaries as clearly as possible, arm staff with the technical and political knowledge required for the job, and get out of their way. If you hired well, then you have intelligent people who are capable of great work and who want to succeed. Let them. Micromanaging will not help them learn for themselves, can undermine their self-worth, and may lead to an unmotivated staff.

With regard to staff: Battling the ever-present temptation to check Twitter and Facebook is a challenge that didn't exist when I began my administrative career. One way to work against the enticements of the social network is to make fun acceptable in the office. This is my fourth lesson.

Yet having a sense of humor is not a license to be cavalier about work. Whether it's loading a new application, registering a student, or filing a grade change request, all of our actions impinge on the integrity of each student record we touch. Take the work seriously; just don't take yourself too seriously. Remember that we were hired to do a job—and that when we are no longer employed in our positions, our job will still get done. There may well be a bump or two before the job is accomplished with the same level of proficiency, but it is possible that a new employee's perspective on our work might bring a better result. Simply stated, no one is irreplaceable.

If you can bring some levity to the work—and even laugh at yourself in the process—your employees will embrace even the most mundane tasks. For example, we key entered more than 500,000 grades in our legacy records system twice in a five-day period. Then we sight verified, line by line, each grade that had been entered. Long hours accepting rosters from faculty members and entering and proofreading seemingly endless data could easily have taken a toll on staff morale and accuracy. To "lighten" the atmosphere, we rented a helium tank and tied a balloon to the chair of each person who went "above and beyond" the call. "Balloon-worthy performance" included finding a mistake in the proofing of grades or entering the fifteen-page grade roster we dreaded each term. The balloons floating above the workstations signaled to everyone that staff members were being recognized for their important contributions to the process. After hours, the administrators would break out bags of marshmallows for a ten-minute marshmallow war. You might be surprised at how much tension can be dispelled by tossing a puffy treat at your boss!

This leads me to my fifth and final point: Remember that you are all in the same office, with the same mission, fighting the same fights. Just as no one person is irreplaceable, so the best successes result from team effort. JR Holmes, the 2009 *USA Today's* National High School Basketball Coach of the Year, said, "You'll be amazed what you can accomplish when you don't care who gets the credit."

Your staff are important, individually and as a collective. Respect the gifts that each brings to the office, support those who need your extra effort, laugh with them, and listen. Each one has an important voice. Give each person the tools you'd like to be given, such as gentle guidance and clear expectations, and then get out of their way. As when your children grow and leave home, you'll be prouder of the accomplishments of your staff than you might imagine. And when you've provided them all the challenges your office has to offer, support their efforts to grow in a new direction. Even if you have to start the process all over again with a new employee, the future success of your staff often lies outside your office's front door.

15

CHAPTER FIFTEEN

The Greatest Gift of All

CLAYTON SMITH

In the final

episode of the Harry Potter movies—*Harry Potter and the Deathly Hallows: Part 2*—Dumbledore tells Harry that "help will always be given at Hogwarts to those who ask for it." He goes on to say, "I've always prided myself in my ability to turn a phrase. But I would, in this case, amend my original statement to this: help will always be given at Hogwarts to those who deserve it." Something between these two statements is probably the truth. At least, that has been my experience in my professional career. The most important thing I have learned is to recognize that I need and deserve help to be successful—and that I need to ask for it often.

Mine has been a career that has included positions in government and higher education, with the last 25 years having been spent working at four postsecondary institutions in the United States and Canada. In all cases (and I mean *all* cases), I have been blessed by having a caring and supportive mentor (sometimes more than one).

As a high school student, I had an incredible history teacher by the name of Mr. Kelley who always took time to talk with my friends and me after school about how history lives in current events. He opened up the excitement of learning in a way that led to an awakening of my intellect and a lifelong thirst for knowledge across academic disciplines.

While in college, I connected with Edwin Pert, who then served as clerk of the Maine House of Representatives. I met Mr. Pert while hitchhiking (it was safe then) to attend extracurricular events. He and I had many conversations about the role of government in changing society and improving the lives of all of us. His down-to-earth communication skills, which were as much about listening as speaking, became the basis of how I relate with peers to this day. Mr. Pert also guided me to staff positions in the Maine House of Representatives and the U.S. Senate.

I was blessed along the way to have had many excellent faculty mentors who gave me the confidence to complete four degrees with a number of work gaps in between. I remember three faculty mentors, in particular: Dr. Oliver Woshinsky shared his faith in the human spirit during many conversations after class; Dr. David Leslie inspired me to think of how I might foster development in the minds and hearts of America's youths; and Dr. Jon Dalton spent countless hours guiding me through the writing of my doctoral dissertation. I truly appreciate the time they took. It made a real difference in my career path.

The first person in my higher education career with whom I connected was Mary Elisabeth Randall, my supervisor at the time and a future president of AACRAO. (I am sure I never would have become active in AACRAO without Mary Elisabeth's support—though she did encourage me to go to my first professional conference on my wife's birthday.) Mary Elisabeth taught me the importance of professional competence and how to work with colleagues in a respectful and honest manner. I will never forget the necessity of doing so.

Mike Bussell, a community college colleague, taught me how to balance the twin responsibilities of creating access for underserved populations (and those for whom postsecondary education is a reach) and maintaining academic quality through decisions made every day. Our frequent lunch conversations demonstrated how this gregarious and thoughtful colleague lived the community college dream and inspired me to embed it in my spirit.

Dr. Kenneth Wing hired me to increase enrollment at an institution that was struggling. What I remember most is his fatherly guidance throughout the challenges. Although he is retired now, he sends holiday updates each year. And when I get back to Maine, we always find time for a meal together. He is just that type of fellow: supportive and caring always.

Professor Neil Gold hired me for my current position at the University of Windsor. He taught me patience; how to find time to listen and time to act; and the importance of internationalizing higher education (which recently has become an important focus of my work).

Two of my current colleagues have left their mark as well: Dr. Alan Wildeman, my current president, connected with me in his first few months on the job when we experienced a faculty strike. He taught me how important it is to reach out to students, parents, and staff during such moments. His calm during periods of crisis is forever in my mind. My current provost, Dr. Leo Groarke, has been instrumental in showing me how to establish priorities so the important work of the university is foremost in my mind. This has been particularly helpful as I balance my twin portfolios of student engagement and internationalization (it is easy to get caught in the "weeds!").

Uncertain as to the particular type of enrollment management practices in place across the Canadian landscape when I first came to work in the country, I sought out a colleague to guide me to a deeper understanding so I might avoid making a few mistakes along the way. Our director of registrarial services told me one day, "You will need to call Susan Gottheil." I learned much from Susan over the years, and my guess is that she learned a few things from me. We have presented together at probably no fewer than 20 conferences;

we started and still serve as co-conveners of the Canadian SEM Summit; we co-managed Canada's online SEM library; and we edited AACRAO's first book on Canadian strategic enrollment management. Ours is a partnership I cherish. (Knowing that we have helped to support the development of SEM in Canada is a thrill!)

I have benefited from the influence of many other mentors. Some have been supervisors, others colleagues in other departments or at other institutions. Some of my most long-lasting mentors have been AACRAO members, and some are AACRAO Consulting colleagues. I remain friends with many of them to this day.

Looking back over my career, I believe that the most important thing I have done as a leader has been to learn from my mentors and to serve as a mentor not only to those with whom I work but also to colleagues throughout my career network. There is nothing more influential than a mentor who knows you, cares about your future, and remains connected to you over an extended period of time.

In recent years, it has been my privilege to serve as a mentor to student government leaders and the leaders of student clubs and societies at the University of Windsor. Some of my most enjoyable moments have transpired during a barbecue at my home when I have listened to the plans of student leaders and have been privileged to help them to their next stop. I am hopeful that I will remain connected to these people throughout their careers. This may be one of the best ways I have found to live out my educational values. I hope to do so for many years to come.

If you are reading this in search of some morsel of wisdom, let me encourage you to first seek out the mentors that are already in your world. They are waiting for you to ask them for help. They have so much to offer! Also consider becoming a mentor yourself (after all, giving is more important than receiving…or, at the least, it is another way of receiving). Don't worry about how experienced you are. One can serve as a mentor at any age and with any amount of experience. It just takes a willingness to share and to enrich those around you. Being a mentor really is the greatest gift of all.

16

CHAPTER SIXTEEN

Leadership and Mentoring for Success

PAUL AND KIM TAYLOR

Chapter Sixteen

Kim and I

were recently driving from Dallas to Austin, where she was to begin a new job as associate registrar at the University of Texas. We had agreed to discuss the subject of this article on the trip, so we talked about our profession; our various jobs; our mutual interest in, love for, and service to our association(s); our mentors; and how we ended up where we are in our respective professional lives. (Good thing it was a long ride!)

We began by acknowledging that most of us don't aspire from a young age to become enrollment managers or registrars or directors of admission and chart a path to carry us to the pinnacle of our profession. Formal training for these positions rarely takes place in a classroom; instead, it typically results from a series of opportunities and events that enable us to learn from a variety of experiences and people. We observe what others are doing well and then try to adapt those best practices to our own environment or situation. We tweak what we learn, add our personal touch (or not), and use it to improve a service or product or to meet a specific need.

One of the most effective venues for learning is the professional association meeting or conference. The reason for attending a conference is to learn. It is one of the great opportunities in our profession. There are ample opportunities to network and socialize, but when my staff attend a conference, the rule is that they can play hard in the evening, but they need to attend sessions during the day.

As Kim and I continued our conversation, we agreed that mentoring and leading are critical to helping individuals reach their goals. Often, the words mentoring and leading are interchangeable. The day after Kim and I arrived in Austin, two things happened that I found particularly thought provoking given our conversation about leadership.

I recently read an article about Ichiro Suzuki, an All Star baseball player for the Seattle Mariners who was traded to the New York Yankees. The article described how the Mariners were better off as a result of the trade. Steve Kelley, of the *Seattle Times,* commented on Suzuki's leadership—or lack thereof. He talked about some of the players on the Mariners' championship team of 2001, when Suzuki was a rookie. Many of the veteran players on the team—Jay Buhner, David Bell, and John Olerud—were leaders and would talk about the nuances of the game for hours on end, helping the young guys learn the ins and outs. "But when it came his [Suzuki's] time to lead, he didn't stay around after games to talk hitting with the younger players, who would have remained in the clubhouse until dawn just to learn some of his baseball secrets (especially hitting). Ichiro never stood up. He never took the heat off some of the younger players by accepting some of the blame as the Mariners faltered over the last couple of years. Imagine the benefit that kind of selflessness could have had on a young Mariners clubhouse," reported Kelley (2012). Consciously or unconsciously, Ichiro Suzuki chose not to be a leader.

Later that same day, a sports reporter announced the Olympic semifinal beach volleyball match featuring April Ross and her partner, Jen Kessy, the eventual silver medal winners. He explained that

Ross begged her parents to let her try out for the volleyball team when she was in the seventh grade. The coach who was at those tryouts told her she had a chance to be really good at the sport.

Here were two opposite examples of leadership: One person, with so much to give, turned his back; the other led just by talking with another.

Both Kim and I could name the mentors who influenced our early careers. Those individuals saw something in each of us that they nurtured, and we, in turn, tried to emulate their behavior. Although we were eager to learn and wanted to succeed, we also didn't want to disappoint them or prove unfounded the confidence they had shown in us.

My first experience in a professional association was as a member of the Kentucky ACRAO Local Arrangements Committee. I won't ever forget the person who asked me to serve in this role. I might never have volunteered on my own, but I knew I would enjoy the experience, and I wanted to do more. (Little did I realize at the time that I eventually would have the opportunity to serve as president of the national association!) Together, KACRAO, SACRAO, and AACRAO provided me the opportunity not only to visit 35 states and four foreign countries but also to mentor individuals along the way.

So how do a man from a mid-sized community college in Kentucky and a woman from a mid-sized state university in Texas end up with the kinds of opportunities we have had? We volunteered for a task and kept on volunteering and serving in any way we could and anytime we were asked. Kim continues to serve as a member of the SACRAO executive committee. She served previously on Texas's N&E Committee and program committees and as president of Kentucky ACRAO and as local arrangements chair for SACRAO.

We both believe that when we volunteered to serve an association, we were making a commitment to follow through with whatever the responsibility required. Volunteering meant giving our time and effort while doing our "regular" full-time jobs. That meant sometimes staying late or working during the evening. But we both were convinced that we got far more out of any volunteer task than we ever put in. What was the reward? We felt good about generating results; often, someone recognized our effort, which meant that we got the chance to volunteer for something else—something new and different. Good leaders not only have to give of their time and talent, but they do so for the betterment of their profession.

As committee chairs and association officers, we had the opportunity to identify and mentor new talent. Through the years, a number of people have told me that they appreciated my helping them achieve their professional or association goals. It was no different on our campuses: I could think of more than a dozen people I should thank one more time for helping me achieve what I have.

At various points in our careers, people helped us to be better managers. They gave us opportunities to try new things, rewarded us for our efforts, and didn't berate us when something failed. We both believe it is important to hire the strongest, smartest, most capable people that can be found. Provide them with the tools they need to do their job, and then get out of their way. Micromanaging has stifled the creativity and performance of many talented individuals.

Help your staff become leaders. Push them in the direction of professional development. Insist that they become involved at the state, regional, or national level. Not all of them will serve someday as state presidents, but many will. The director of admissions, director of financial aid, and registrar who reported to me at Lexington Community College all served as presidents of their Kentucky professional associations. As often as the opportunity arises, recognize these individuals in front of faculty or peers for the work they do. Give them credit for all of their successes, and privately assure them that you will stand with them even if they make a mistake—to fix the problem, help them learn from it, and ensure that it doesn't happen again. People will respond to this type of leadership the same way you would. Those who approach us as "us" or as "team" are the ones for whom we will do anything.

A good leader can admit to a subordinate that her idea is better than his. A good leader can make mistakes, and a good leader can fail. A good leader who errs will stand tall and admit his mistake. And a leader will not lose sight of the goal; she will take the team's suggestions and contributions and make the whole stronger than its parts. (Imagine Peyton Manning with no receivers!)

Kim and I both have had supervisors who were good leaders. Unwavering in their pursuit of specific goals, they nevertheless equipped us with the tools we needed. Perhaps more important, they had the self-confidence to allow us the flexibility to do our work our way. They were our supervisors, but they viewed us as colleagues and teammates working to achieve the same goal. They were ready to assist us if we needed them to, but they served more as coaches and teachers who helped us succeed. We would have gone as far as was humanly possible to make sure our leader's goals were realized.

I have long been personally committed to providing people with opportunities to serve and/or to be recognized at the state, regional, and national levels. During my tenure on the AACRAO board, I wanted people who didn't know anyone (that is, they were not part of the group that would have access) to be able to submit a program session for the annual meeting or to volunteer to serve. Admittedly, this was partly because of Kim. I knew her to be a strong registrar at a regional college in Texas, and I knew she was completely capable of presenting a program at the annual meeting. But how could someone from a small community college in Kentucky or even a regional state university in Texas advance a program topic to the regional or national level? To me, being a leader in AACRAO meant finding a way for such individuals to accomplish this; we did so by opening program planning to the membership. This is one of the accomplishments of which I am most proud.

It is important to foster leadership in persons different from yourself. At a recent presentation, they showed a picture of the board of directors. The picture might as well have been taken in 1950: seven white males, all over the age of 50, stared back at me. I have strived throughout my career to ensure that women and minorities were given chances to demonstrate and build their leadership skills. It is so important for the young people in our profession to look at their organizational leaders and see people like themselves serving in primary roles. When they see association officers like themselves, they know that they, too, can aspire to be leaders. I was proud to have been on the boards of directors of both SACRAO and AACRAO when leadership positions were established to represent minorities.

In all likelihood, you know if you are a leader, and you know that you can have great influence on those around you. Take the responsibility seriously, and provide guidance and opportunities to those who seek such. Always keep in mind that people in your organization and on your campus and in your professional association are watching what you do and how you do it. I'm reminded of the Blake Shelton song "Who Are You When I'm Not Looking?"

People observe the way you are dressed; they see if you are monitoring your e-mail or texting during meetings; they even observe how you interact with others in the room. Your posture, your eye contact, your body language speak volumes.

If you aspire to become a leader, find a mentor to help you get to where you want to go. Find someone you can talk to, brainstorm with, and get ideas from. If you are in the position to be that leader and a mentor, spend time and effort to help those who can benefit from your guidance and wisdom. Serving as a mentor and leader will ensure that the return on your investment will be immeasurable.

17

CHAPTER SEVENTEEN

Leadership: Principle Driven Action

ROGER J. THOMPSON

In thinking

about strategic enrollment management (SEM), it seems appropriate to refer to one of the long-standing texts in the field. In *The Strategic Management of College Enrollments,* Hossler and Bean and Associates (1990) provide a four-part overview of how to create a strong SEM organization on campus.

The book's four areas of focus are enrollment management in academic settings, the marketing dimension of enrollment management, student retention in enrollment management, and building comprehensive enrollment management systems. Hossler and Bean provide a thorough overview of the field and also provide case studies. The higher education landscape quickly adapted as enrollment challenges emerged and as enrollment management practices became more widespread, having begun to be developed first at Boston College and then at Bradley University.

Today, the term "enrollment management" is common on many college campuses, and the support network for SEM professionals ranges from publications to conferences, institutes, and continuing education programs. One could argue that enrollment management "has arrived" in the higher education community and that the discussion now has turned from the foundational structures of forming enrollment management organizations to how to effectively lead such organizations.

It is a compliment to our profession that we now are examining not only the key components Hossler, Bean, and others have addressed through several decades of research and publications but also how leadership contributes to successful enrollment management.

Thinking about leadership and about how one becomes an effective leader naturally includes a review of the literature. The number of outstanding authors and publications on leadership is virtually endless, but without fail, I return to Warren Bennis and his writings. His text *On Becoming a Leader* (1989) is classic. In fact, Bennis provides perhaps the best guide to being successful as a leader of an enrollment management organization.

That said, among the names that come to mind regarding leadership in enrollment management are not only Bennis and John Gardner (1990) but also Berra—as in *Yogi* Berra. Many may not think of Lawrence Peter "Yogi" Berra as an authority on leadership, though he did have a successful major league baseball career as catcher and manager for the New York Yankees; instead, he is best known for his mishandling of the English language. A true leader in the field of enrollment management, David Kalsbeek once quoted Yogi Berra: "When you come to a fork in the road, take it!"

This may best describe a leadership style long ignored but vitally important.

As an invited lecturer to a graduate student course on strategic enrollment management, I once was asked to describe my leadership style. After a long pause, I offered the idea that mine was the Yogi Berra leadership style. The students roared with laughter, and I chuckled and smiled. Then I began to describe leadership and why Yogi Berra's quotation about the fork in the road might describe a leadership quality that is critical to success. The underlying message of this quote is to take action; after all, action is critical to leadership.

I refer to this quotation for two reasons: First, it always gets a laugh, which cannot be under-valued given the challenges confronting higher education and society today. Second, and more important, the key to leadership is action, though it sometimes is the most overlooked leadership trait. The most recent literature about leadership includes plenty of discussion about listening, being participative, engaging key stake-holders, utilizing data, conducting research, and more. But not enough is written about *acting*—not in the George Clooney sense but rather as a leader who makes decisions. In other words, it is critical to get to the decision point and make one. This is what leaders do—ideally, with a strategic sense of where they wish to lead their organizations.

To paraphrase Woodrow Wilson, "A leader's ears must always ring with the voices of his constituents." This quotation is another personal favorite because it asserts the importance of connecting with key constituencies and being an engaged and active listener. The statement also speaks to the idea of servant leadership (if long before that term was widely discussed or published). One also needs to remember that after hearing the voices of the constituents, the leader must act and move with decisiveness to meet their needs. Leadership does not happen without action.

Enrollment management organizations often are driven either by crisis or by a specific challenge that may be affecting revenues adversely (Hossler and Bean 1990). In such circumstances, leadership is even more critical.

In the course of leading a number of enrollment management organizations and trying to increase my own leadership abilities, I have learned that the leader must support core concepts critical to organizational success. Where core principles of excellence are absent, the organization will not achieve its full potential; in such circumstances, it is critical for the leader to provide the guidance necessary to create a successful organization built on core principles.

At the University of Oregon, these principles revolve around the student life cycle. The life cycle begins at the time the institution first interacts with a student (or family) as a prospect, defined here as having an interest in the institution, or as a "suspect." Suspects are students of interest to the institution who may not yet be aware of the institution. In any event, the life cycle begins with the prospect stage and concludes when students become alumni and, ultimately, donors. Becoming a donor is the most important measure of alumni satisfaction; the individual who is willing to donate time, energy, goodwill, or money demonstrates a significant level of alumni satisfaction.

The core principles of successful organizations are similar to those described in the research but are described here in a slightly different form. Successful organizations demonstrate a commitment to these organizational principles:

- Constituent focused;
- Strategic;
- Flexible and nimble;
- Energetic;
- Empowered;
- Team oriented; and
- Communication focused.

To comment briefly on each of these qualities is appropriate given that leaders (in my view, at least) must embrace and create organizations that are strong in each of these areas.

To be "constituent focused" begins with acknowledging that successful enrollment management organizations serve many constituents, including students, parents, faculty, staff, alumni, government officials, and community members, among others. A natural commitment to service emerges when constituents and their needs are placed at the center of the work. This is crucial for any organization, but it is critical for an enrollment management organization. Taking pride in serving others and being a model in this regard are key components of a strong organization.

It is hard to imagine that any successful organization is not also strategic, but this is critical in enrollment management organizations. Focusing on student recruitment and retention and how the size, quality, diversity, internationality, and other characteristics of the student body affect the institution and the broader community and society is imperative. Enrollment management must be strategic. Given the financial challenges confronting so many institutions in today's economy, a strategic approach across the various departments involved in enrollment management is fundamental to success. The marketplace for students is changing, so an effective leader must constantly ask how the organization and service "fit." This is strategic thinking: Continual assessment of marketplace "match" is a fundamental role of the talented enrollment management leader.

Organizations must be flexible and nimble if they are to be successful. This is challenging for institutions of any size, but it becomes more challenging as the scale increases. Leaders must be able to adapt and be nimble as the marketplace, constituent expectations, technology, demographics, and many other factors change rapidly. Finding solutions and moving with agility is difficult in any organization, but the leader must be willing and ready to move quickly when the opportunity to do so arises.

When one considers the role of the registrar's office just fifteen to twenty years ago, the argument for flexibility and nimbleness becomes self-evident. Consider a financial aid office where new federal regulations virtually require a system migration every year. If the leader operates in this manner, the rest of the organization will follow. Leaders must find solutions; often, this requires being creative, but most important, it requires taking action once a solution has been identified.

Leaders and successful organizations must have energy. The leader needs to bring enthusiasm, excitement, and energy to everything he does—which, in turn, results in the organization itself being energetic. Demonstrating energy and enthusiasm has taken many forms over the course of my career. Years ago, we set some lofty enrollment goals. The team was enthusiastic, and during a fairly routine meeting, I was asked whether we might celebrate with a cruise if we met the new goals. Everyone laughed—myself included—but months later, when the goal had been met, I arranged for the entire organization to set sail on a cruise... on the river that ran through town! Never mind that the "cruise ship" was a local paddle-wheeled boat and that the cruise lasted for hours instead of days. The method may have been unorthodox, but the energy and enthusiasm it generated throughout our organization was noticeable. The message to the team was important, on many levels.

Tenacity and energy move organizations forward; at most successful organizations, the leader plays a critical role in unleashing energy in pursuit of institutional goals. I cannot understate the importance of energy and commitment during the course of my own career. Significant change in an institution usually relates to the energetic approach of the leader. Establishing lofty goals and objectives—even those which may seem out of reach—and then accomplishing them generates an incredible feeling within an organization. I have said for years that if you could imbue middle school kids with the feeling of accomplishment that accompanies the attainment of lofty, far-reaching goals, we would not have many of the problems that we have in society today. (In truth, I'm not sure the solution is quite that easy or straight-forward, though I believe it would be a great place to start.) The point is that organizations reflect their leaders: Creating organizations that are based on energy will always serve them well.

When I was in graduate school, a professor argued that the best decisions are made closest to the contact point. Experience has made me believe this all the more. Empowering others is a key leadership trait. One can only accomplish so much individually; but once an organization's people are empowered, the level of excellence increases.

A few years ago, at another institution, we created an entirely new department designed to meet a series of enrollment goals. I vividly recall the wonderful conversation I shared with the director about how the department would take form, the type of work that would be accomplished, and the difference the department would make to our larger organization and to the university as a whole. I encouraged the director to create, to be imaginative, and to develop the department in accordance with her unique leadership style. I referred to the department as a blank canvas and paints and urged the director to create a masterpiece. In other words, I utilized the leadership principle of hiring the right people; giving them the tools, knowledge, skills, abilities, and support to be successful; and then getting out of the way so they can create the magic. It is important to support and to provide assistance when needed, but if you do your job, your newly empowered leader will develop her own skills and deliver results. This is empowerment. The results will be wonderful and will include the person becoming a better leader and the organization being better served.

Encouraging initiative and empowerment results in productivity gains and efficiencies. After all, who knows better how to solve a problem than the person closest to it? Through empowerment, the organization itself becomes energized. These two principles support one another.

When one thinks broadly about organizational principles, it becomes apparent that these last two principles—encouraging initiative and empowerment—are critical to those described earlier. Building a team and ensuring effective communication cut across the other areas to support the rest of the principles. Further, each of the aforementioned principles interacts with the others, though communication and a sense of team may do so in a more unique manner. To build a sense of team, a leader must establish trust, cohesion, and common goals and support and reward effective team members. Team building is described throughout the literature on leadership. Yet the reality of team building typically is complicated; rarely does the new leader get to hire all of the members of the team. The challenge often is to build trust and cohesion where they may not have existed previously. This can be challenging. In *Strengths Based Leadership,* the authors state, "Effective leaders surround themselves with the right people and build on each person's strength" (Rath and Conchie 2008). Intuitively, we know this, but the leadership challenge is to build the team when the majority of its members are inherited.

Leadership cannot be nurtured either individually or organizationally without strong communication. A leader must support effective communication systems through hard work and constant monitoring of the organization. Effective communication enables and supports all of the other principles of good leadership. Without strong communication, there is no foundation on which to build. Communication also is critical if one is to move students through the life cycle and serve key constituents effectively. Seamless service does not happen without a strong organizational foundation, of which communication is the building block.

These organizational principles must be supported by the leader if the organization is to develop and attain new heights. Certainly, there are other critical factors, such as strong strategic planning processes, clearly articulated and understood goals and objectives, measures of progress and re-assessment, modification and adjustment based on a culture of continuous organizational assessment. But the organization can never fully reach its potential if it fails to establish its core principles. To reach that potential, one must act, and that brings us back full circle to the leadership style I offer for consideration—that of one Lawrence Peter "Yogi" Berra: "When you come to a fork in the road, take it." In the context of leadership, that means that when action is required, the leader must act.

18

CHAPTER EIGHTEEN

Hit the Ground Listening

SUSAN VAN VOORHIS

I never really

thought about my leadership style until six years ago. My goal for the office then—as now—was to make a difference for students, faculty, and staff in the university community. At the time, everyone talked about the baby boomers' retiring and taking undocumented knowledge with them. After learning that 58 percent of my staff soon would be eligible to retire (though I still had a long way to go), I knew it was important to ensure that the organization remained strong for students, faculty, and staff, despite the changes that lay ahead. Our unit, Academic Support Resources (ASR), has been called the central nervous system, the backbone, and the infrastructure of the university. Considering this responsibility and the potential loss of dedicated, knowledgeable staff, it was clear that we needed an organizational effectiveness plan to secure "the infrastructure" of the University. Carefully honed guidance played a distinctive role in orchestrating the plan, and my personal leadership journey has been defined largely by its development.

CREATING THE MISSION, VISION, AND VALUES

The ASR unit directors and I realized that the office's mission, vision, and values needed to align more clearly with the University of Minnesota's own purpose of instruction, research, and outreach. A cross-unit and cross-staff development team was created and charged with two tasks: providing preliminary feedback on a mission and vision statement developed by myself and the ASR directors and organize an all-staff event during which employees would provide feedback on our initial statements. At the first event, all staff were assigned to tables (yes, we assigned seats) to create additional cross-functional and cross-staff groups; reactions to the mission and vision were gathered through targeted questions. As part of an "ice breaker," each group also answered questions regarding what they valued about working for ASR and the University. Subsequent analysis of this information was displayed in seven affinity diagrams.

The team continued to meet and communicate with directors to determine how best to refine our mission and vision. Ultimately, it was the team's draft, based on feedback from all ASR staff, that informed the unit's current mission and vision. The team then determined how best to communicate the themes of the affinity diagrams in relatively short statements. These ultimately became our organizational values. Our mission, vision, and values are now incorporated into the annual review process. This ensures that their importance is understood.

Each year, we form a development team that focuses on creating two all-staff events. The resultant team-building contributes to the department's overall success. For example, I give a yearly "state of ASR" address to inform staff of upcoming goals, changes, and other important information. Staff are willing to assist and provide feedback to strengthen the organization when they feel empowered through this sharing of information.

A STAFF-FOCUSED ORGANIZATIONAL EFFECTIVENESS PLAN

We adopted an organizational effectiveness plan as part of our effort to keep the office strong as we head into the future and 'live' our mission—"to make a positive difference in students' lives"—and our vision—"to foster student success." Rather than focusing simply on business processes or service automation, ASR's plan focuses primarily on staff; ultimately, they are responsible for the success of the office.

As the directors and I developed the plan, it became clear that we had a significant amount of work to do to ensure the unit's long-term success. First, we worked to identify gaps in the organization's knowledge, skills, and abilities. We compiled information—about staff members' current needs; we reviewed job descriptions; and we researched similar positions. This helped us to detail the knowledge, skills, and abilities (KSA) required for each position. We then grouped jobs according to their KSAs. Seven "career families" emerged from these groupings. Next we assigned staff to the "career family" that most closely matched their position. The resultant 'families' were cross-functional as well as cross–staff level. (Because many staff could work well within several of the career families, assignments were based on the KSAs required for at least 51 percent of their work) That said, the same KSAs are not repeated across multiple families; rather, those that are required of every position reflect our organizational values. In other words, certain behaviors demonstrate our values, with the result that staff now know "what it looks like" when they are "going above and beyond." The career families have allowed us to utilize staff across units in different situations. For example, when a staff member left our fiscal unit, we were able to make use of resources in our accounting unit until the position in the fiscal unit was filled.

Because it was particularly important for staff members to understand the unit's direction and goals—to include the role of *expectations* in its success—we communicated the organizational effectiveness plan in several ways. A significant component of the plan focuses on staff development. Because employees make or break the organization's success, I meet with each new employee and explain the organizational effectiveness plan in depth. I describe the office and our budget, but I focus primarily on my expectations of employees as leaders. Afterward, our coordinator of organizational effectiveness describes the plan in even greater detail. It is at this meeting that prospective employees are introduced to the career families and the resources provided for individual development. Once these meetings have been completed, new employees have a thorough understanding of their roles within the context of the organizational effectiveness plan. Each employee should be a leader by taking responsibility for her own development.

WHAT DO I MEAN BY "LEADER?"

The expectation is that each employee will be the best person in her position as she strives to meet the leadership expectation depicted in Figure 1. Specifically, each employee is accountable for her actions, development, and longevity in the position. Supervisors are accountable for the middle column in addition to the first, and unit directors are expected to adhere to all that is listed. Employee leadership is completely self-driven and supervisor assisted. Each staff member creates an Individualized Development Plan (IDP) and shares it with her supervisor. If a staff member wishes to increase her proficiency or to learn new skills so she can apply for another position in the office, the supervisor is expected to help her locate resources accordingly (within reason). That said, we strive to hire the best-qualified person—internal candidate or external—for every position. The organizational effectiveness plan, which we have

FIGURE 1. ASR LEADERSHIP SKILLS AND ABILITIES

Leadership (All ASR Staff)	Leadership (Supervisors)	Leadership (Directors)
Contribute	Lead People	Lead organization and multiple direct reports
Manage individual performance	Optimize system performance	Accountable for organizational performance
Support sound decisions	Make sound decisions	Use astute judgment
Understand strategy	Think and act strategically	Shape strategy
Align actions with unit and ASR goals	Support unit and ASR goals	Accountable for setting unit and ASR goals
Mindfully use allocated resources	Strategically request and manage resources	Strategically allocate resources
Learn from actions	Think innovatively	Display vision
Influence productivity	Maintain enterprise-wide perspective	Drive enterprise-wide perspective
Seek customer satisfaction	Meet customer needs	Ensure customer and stakeholder focus
Implement effective plans	Build realistic plans	Align the organization (within ASR and to the U)
Take initiative	Take initiative	Drive organizational success
Weigh risks of alternative actions	Manage risks	Lead the organization with levelheaded confidence
Support colleagues	Build support	Use organizational influence
Energize the workplace	Create engaging environment	Energize the organization
Develop self and support others	Develop and support direct reports	Develop, support, and motivate staff throughout the organization
Be a team player	Promote teamwork	Ensure collaboration
Represent ASR values in all interactions	Build organizational relationships	Safeguard and strengthen organizational relationships
Earn respect	Earn trust	Maintain and grow trusted relationships
Help resolve issues during crisis/team issues	Help resolve issues during crisis/system issues	Create strategies to anticipate and prevent system issues
Be a "green" individual	Be a "green" manager	Be a "green" leader
Be an effective active listener	Be an effective internal communicator	Be an expert internal and external communicator
Actively Participate in training	Perform training	Set training goals

posted on our intranet, permits us to post only internally (it is worth noting that for some openings, our organization has many qualified internal candidates). In my opinion, this means our plan is successful. The same is true of staff who are content in their current positions: It is their responsibility to work with their supervisor to ensure their continued success, which may require keeping up with technology and improving business processes for greater efficiencies. This portion of the plan is driven by the employee but supervisor assisted.

The organizational effectiveness team continues to evaluate the strength of the organization and to implement changes necessary to meet the evolving needs of the University community. These changes are always communicated through several channels, *e.g.*, a newsletter, director's e-mail, brown-bag lunches on specific topics, and all-staff events. Supervisors are expected to answer staff members' questions and to seek answers from the unit director as necessary. This is done in combination with ongoing communication of the mission, vision, and goals of the unit as well as any pending initiatives. Staff who understand the unit's goals and outcomes are confident in themselves and their achievement; ultimately, this contributes to the success of the unit. Staff must be treated well. When the directors and I are thanked for the work we do, we immediately attribute our success to the staff. The provost once asked me, "How do you manage to accomplish so much for the University?" I replied that it wasn't me but the great staff who was accomplishing so much, and then I thanked him. This is the type of leadership style I prefer: aligning and communicating goals and removing barriers that inhibit staff performance.

Although this plan was created about six years ago, it is a continuous process. I am not interested in a succession plan that specifies that a person in a particular position will take over when someone else leaves. Rather, I always try to hire the best person for the position and to give all qualified staff the opportunity to apply. When we first started to create our organizational effectiveness plan, we created a team that visited several companies in the Minneapolis area to gather as much information as possible. We wanted to be sure that we considered all possible pieces of a plan so we would be in alignment with the University.

Another area on which we have focused is supervisor development. A small team of ASR volunteer staff conducts an anonymous quarterly employee survey. Suggestions are consistently made with regard to supervising. Early discussions made it apparent that we had a wide range of expectations of our supervisors. To promote consistency, supervisors now meet on a regular basis—about once every two months. Agenda items include supervisor expectations, evaluation of the performance review process, management of employee situations—positive and negative, organizational change, and professional development and employee checklists. Supervisors no longer simply supervise; many are also performing specific tasks. It is crucial to ensure that supervisors understand leadership and how to support employees so the unit can maximize its success. Routine employee surveys help me understand how employees perceive themselves within the organization; this, too, is critical to the unit's success.

SETTING ORGANIZATIONAL GOALS

I have been in my current position for about ten years. As I reflect on my conduct when I first started in the office, I realize I could have been a much better leader. At the time, we were completing a student system conversion; implementing a one-stop student services model; creating an office of classroom management; combining student finance and financial aid units; converting to semesters; and transitioning administrations. All went well, thanks to a dedicated staff who lacked the benefit of guidance from their leader. I should have set goals, sought input, and communicated with staff. Instead, I maintained a breakneck pace and struggled against feeling overwhelmed. Today, the projects remain numerous; but one significant difference is that the organizational effectiveness plan requires that we set goals for staff to work toward. This ensures that we all head in the same direction as we adhere to the same mission. We now are able to respond both to emergencies and to new initiatives identified by the administration, and this makes everyone's job easier. We accomplished this with a team of dedicated leaders who truly value student success.

I have never considered myself the type of leader to dictate what must occur. To be honest, I don't consider myself a leader but rather a facilitator and barrier breaker. I prefer to listen, gather goals from the broader community, and determine direction with guidance and feedback from the administration, colleges, and coordinate campuses. I prefer to rely on consensus or buy-in from the majority to ensure success. Those of us in student services are lucky because we can witness first-hand the achievements that result from our positions. This is gratifying. When a decision must be made, I can make the wisest choice thanks to the information my staff provide. Team discussion and debate are both encouraged and welcomed.

If a team member thinks only of the unit he supervises, you will need to address the situation. Neither your organization nor staff will attain success if such a narrow focus is not broadened. How the individual is approached will prove critical. In my own experience, I work with the employee to develop an appropriate plan for meeting the challenge at hand. This acknowledges the delicacy of the situation and keeps the organization moving forward.

Other key ingredients of a unit's success are integrity, honesty, humility, and a sense of humor. While the truth may hurt, it must be told, or other problems will arise. Ultimately, honesty must prove the order of the day so the unit can accomplish its work. Maturity and pragmatism are essential. Take missteps in stride. Focus on your mission and how to continue to move the organization forward. Also realize that change requires collaborative negotiation. A hostile takeover is never good for staff. Changes need to be negotiated.

THOUGHTS ON LEADERSHIP

Be open and honest when sharing ideas, potential visions, or possible priorities and strategies. Building relationships (especially with the chief financial officer) is critical. Recognize that you are new to the position and that listening and learning are crucial aspects of your work. Create a few high-level talking points and encourage feedback. At an open forum, a potential supervisor once presented her mission, vision, and values along with a proposed organizational chart. It did not go very well for her because she had no idea what offices or functions she would be overseeing. So hit the ground listening and learning as much as possible about the organization—and take copious notes. You'll need to determine what is valuable and informative and what is merely complaining and whining. Assess the pool of talent that is available, and identify where additional knowledge, skills, and abilities may be needed. Assess different cultures within the organization in order to determine how much work needs to be done to build a successful, nimble organization. Multiple cultures within the unit may impede progress. Address issues early by communicating clearly about where the organization is headed. Doing so will help build a strong, cohesive unit. Realize that you have an important opportunity to assess the organization from your perspective. Openness and honesty with staff will cultivate a dedicated team that focuses on and produces for the university.

Gathering information will enable you to build relationships that in turn will help you identify a vision and strategies for attaining it. Leadership means helping others or enhancing a larger goal. Be sure you know the goals of the administration so that yours align. I recall that in first grade, my classmates and I all had to run for "president for a day." My classmates talked about what they would do for the class; I asked what my classmates would like to have happen if I were president for a day. After gathering their suggestions, we voted on the top ten items; the top five became my platform for "president for a day." This worked well: I did not have to talk in front of the class (I was terrified to do so); I had only to listen, take notes, add votes, and read the top five. Perfect! Initially surprised that I won the election, I suddenly realized that now I had to follow through on my commitment. I asked for volunteers, who were happy to contribute to events that were "by and for" the class, not the president. Moreover, the teacher—our top administrator—agreed to our top five, with the result that her goals and our goals mirrored one another. By merely gathering information, I was able to make others happy. Then, as now, I found this much more gratifying than setting an agenda built solely on my own ideas.

Another way in which ASR enables staff to provide feedback and information is by holding "Sue for a day" brown-bag lunches. Staff may discuss anything they wish, to include raising any question. Great ideas evolve from these sessions, and follow-up sessions are scheduled to address what has been accomplished and what items remain pending. I hold brown-bag lunches during which I explain the budget process and my philosophy in ensuring the unit's stability. By listening, knowing limits, and setting clear expectations, almost everyone can move ahead with shared understanding.

Some leaders conceive of their ideas and goals without any staff input whatsoever. Ask yourself, "Who is this for?" Leaders must attract followers to complete a project, but it's imperative for the project to serve the greater good. Leadership is *not* having subordinates do as they're told; that is managing. Managers hold positions of authority and strive to run well-oiled shops; yet many avoid conflict altogether. This type of management can result in a unit becoming stagnant and unsuccessful. ASR staff are responsible for keeping the unit—as well as the University—running well. Every position is important and serves key functions that influence other positions. Indeed, our external impact and gratification keep us energized and focused. As Abraham Lincoln said, "A leader is best when people barely know he exists; when his work is done, his aim fulfilled, they will say we did it ourselves."

How does one work with a leader who builds her own ego and fails to consider the mission of the university? It's not easy. Strive to earn the respect and support of the people in positions of authority above you. As a leader of a unit, you must eliminate barriers so staff can concentrate fully on their responsibilities and the mission of the unit. Exercise care in dealing with contentious and/or political issues. Your success may be threatened if you fail to meet another unit's demand. Keep those in positions of authority informed, and ask how they wish you to handle the situation. Try to negotiate a balance, and do not get caught off guard. If contentious situations continue to arise and impede progress, then it may be time to consider other possibilities. Other AACRAO members will help you conduct a reality check. The demands may be so overwhelming that you need to be assured that you haven't lost your mind. Consider the pros and cons of the situation: Is the unit's mission no longer in alignment with that of the university? Analyzing and adjusting to changing initiatives is common in our profession. And knowing the point at which *you* must adjust is a sign of a strong leader. I often remind staff that we need to return to our unit "bubble" in which our aim is to provide positive outcomes for students, faculty, and staff. Look out for one another and provide guidance and assistance when needed. Finally, be sure to take advantage of opportunities for professional development. Our positions are demanding, and there is no shame in seeking the advice of others.

At the end of the day, passion and fantastic staff fuel success. As John Maxwell once said, "A leader leads by example, whether he intends to or not." My job is to remove obstacles and barriers that impede my staff's success. I want to build confidence in them so they can increase their personal impact on the University, as well as on our overarching mission, which is to make a positive difference in students' lives.

19

CHAPTER NINETEEN

So, You Want To Be A Leader

J. JAMES WAGER

A great many

books, monographs, and articles have been written on the subject of leadership. A Google search of the word returns nearly a half-billion websites. Given this wealth of information, what is the added value of an additional commentary on the subject? I leave the answer to the reader.

As a professional who has spent nearly 40 years in the higher education sector, I have been blessed with opportunities to view and practice leadership from various perspectives: as a staffer at an academic college, as an information technology practitioner, as registrar at a large public university, as a university administrator, as a classroom instructor, and most recently as an executive of a for-profit company. While each of these assignments has had its unique roles and responsibilities, leadership has been a common thread.

Each of us has spheres of influence—opportunity to have an impact on the lives of others. Our roles as parent, spouse, and friend and as manager, co-worker, supplier, and consumer attest to our spheres of influence and our leadership opportunities.

Leadership is not management; we must be careful not to confuse the two. Good managers may be good leaders, but one can be a manager without having followers. Whereas managers have the power and authority to require desired behavior, leaders have the opportunity to make a difference in people's lives and for the organization. The formal authority of a manager enables coercion or even discipline if instructions are not obeyed. Leaders create outcomes such that followers choose to participate in strengthening the organization. Managers are appointed; leaders are identified by their followers. The difference is significant.

We all have leaders in our lives to whom we relate and from whom we learn. I am fortunate to have followed many talented leaders; one was my grandfather. As a young teenager, I was proud of his position: a senior executive at General Electric. As he led me on a tour of the plant, employees were quick to acknowledge his authority. My read was that my grandpa was the man! I felt like a big shot because I was with a big shot. When a man who appeared to be a janitor extended his hand, my grandfather extended his hand in turn, introduced me, entered into a brief conversation, and, upon leaving, tipped his hat to the man. I asked my grandfather why he had done that. His answer surprised me, and it left a lasting impression. He said, "I refuse to let any man be more of a gentleman than I should be myself." This was, for me, an early lesson in leadership.

As they work within their spheres of influence, leaders demonstrate five characteristics: discipline, humility, accountability, perseverance, and vision.

DISCIPLINE

Discipline is doing what has to be done; doing it when it has to be done; and doing it continuously. This is the no excuse zone.

Each day in the registrar's office, we received many phone calls. Our goal was to answer each call personally and to provide an accurate and professional response. To achieve this goal, each staff member (including the registrar) had a weekly "appointment" for "phone duty." This practice was not well received by all staff; some believed they had more important duties to perform.

Among the questions asked most often was, "How do I obtain a copy of my transcript?" The answer to this question was clearly stated on our website; one was tempted to wonder why the caller hadn't first checked their website. After responding to the same question for the umpteenth time, why not cut the caller off and refer him to the website? The answer was simple: Each caller was seeking information and neither knew nor cared that others had asked the same question.

Why were all staff, including the registrar, required to spend time each week answering the phone? The answer was that no task was more important than providing excellent customer service. The discipline required to maintain this perspective was critical to successful leadership. Every time a staff member—regardless of her title—answered the phone, she was "the registrar" representing the university.

Being disciplined requires having a work ethic. As a little league coach, I told my players, "You'll play like you practice." Some got it, and some didn't. It was not uncommon for a boy or girl with average skills to become an outstanding player; unfortunately, it also was not uncommon for a talented youngster to never amount to much of an athlete. Leaders in the workplace must promote these same qualities and work ethic.

HUMILITY

My dad used to tell me that the longer I went to school, the less smart I became. He meant that I should not let my formal education—"book learning"— get in the way of common sense.

To be a leader, one must be humble. People who forsake humility often find themselves in positions of compromise. Arrogance diminishes perspective and distorts reality. Humility keeps us teachable and helps us learn.

Leaders cannot demand respect; they must earn it. Leaders need to demonstrate that the direction, goals, and actions being proposed are best for the organization and for all individuals involved. Confidence is important; arrogance crosses the line. Be humble.

ACCOUNTABILITY

As a result of my professional position, I meet many people. Often, I meet people who want to blame someone for something. Of course, they never consider that they themselves may be part of the problem, let alone that they may be the problem. They don't want to be held accountable for their actions, for their lack of planning, for their misjudgment, etc. Instead, they want someone else to be accountable and to rectify what they deem an unsatisfactory situation.

How often do we read about celebrities, politicians, sports figures, and businessmen who put themselves ahead of the law? Their attitude is that they are not accountable to their fans, constituents, or customers. Rather, they believe that their status affords them special privileges—as if "some are more equal than others." Of course, this is never true.

Yet it is an easy trap for a leader to fall into. Formal authority and associated power may blur the distinction between management and leadership roles. But this is no excuse. Many leaders—myself included—have found they are not fully accountable for every decision. The acid test may be to present the following question to the person (or persons) you most respect: "Would you approve if I were to...?" If the answer is "yes," then your accountability level likely is very high.

I believe that we reap what we sow: No one else is responsible for the leader each of us becomes.

PERSEVERANCE

I have come to appreciate (and have shared often with my son, a Division I-A pitcher) the saying that "pitchers are like tea bags: You never know how strong they are until you put them in hot water."

We are familiar with such one-liners as:

- "If you can't stand the heat, get out of the kitchen."
- "When the going gets tough, the tough get going."
- "Marines do more before breakfast than most people do all day."

Their common theme is work hard and persevere.

Throughout my career, I have been presented with wonderful opportunities to make a difference in people's lives. But never were these opportunities without challenges. Making a difference typically involves change. And change almost always is met with resistance. People fear the unknown; they may believe they no longer will be needed or that they no longer will be capable of fulfilling their responsibilities; they may be convinced that change is unnecessary; and on and on. The successful leader is adept at ushering in change without being confrontational.

One memorable change occurred while I was at Penn State: The university had an established process by which students could withdraw voluntarily from degree status. The process was intended to advise the student of the consequences (academic, financial, and personal) of removing himself from degree status; the practice, unfortunately, was reduced to obtaining multiple signatures on a student action form. Using technology that interacted with the student on a personal and data-driven level, the signature-collection process was replaced with a computer-aided withdrawal process. Student retention increased nearly 10 percent. Ultimately, the new process proved a great success. But prior to and during the change, resistance was great. The nay-sayers argued that personal interaction would be sacrificed, and students would make uninformed decisions. Had the leader of this change lacked conviction, the ability to demonstrate and discuss the change, and commitment to persevere under pressure, this particular improvement would never have been realized.

Michael Jordan is considered by many to be one of the greatest basketball players ever to have worn an NBA jersey. Despite his success, he had to persevere in the face of great competitive pressure. Michael Jordan missed the basket 9,000 times; he lost almost 300 games; 26 times, he was trusted to take the game-winning shot—and missed. Yet he persevered and led his team (his sphere of influence) to many impressive victories.

'VISION

"If you do what you've done, you'll get what you got." People and organizations are prone to get caught in the "lack-of-vision rut," for which they pay a steep price. There are dozens of examples of leaders who lost their vision for their organization, with the result that the organization failed:

- Kodak lost its premier standing in the photography business because its leadership didn't believe that digital cameras would last.
- IBM, which once controlled the computer market, missed the vision that desktop computers would play a significant role.
- The U. S. auto industry just barely re-invented itself so as to remain competitive with foreign manufacturers.
- The U.S. education sector is still trying to determine the role of for-profit education.
- Borders closed hundreds of stores in part because it failed to prepare for the e-book revolution.

Yet there are as many examples of leaders who cast a new vision such that their organizations prospered:

- The cell phone industry quickly surpassed the traditional land-line business.
- Bottled water quickly became one of the most profitable products for many beverage companies.

The list goes on.

Leaders think strategically and demonstrate entrepreneurship. In recent years, higher education administration—and the office of the registrar, in particular—has changed dramatically. The fundamental services they provide—*e.g.*, scheduling courses and classrooms, registering students, recording grades and generating transcripts, managing graduation processes, etc.—remain the same. But vision and entrepreneurship have changed the manner in which these services are delivered. Leaders have a profound impact on their organizations as they challenge the traditional methods by which services, processes, products, and outcomes are achieved. Leaders do not accept the argument that "we have always done it that way." Strategic visioning leads to new and different—and desirable—end points; improvements are not merely incremental but constitute new directions. Whereas managers focus on processes, leaders envision opportunities. They are action driven. As they cast the vision, their fundamental objective is to have followers embrace it. The person whose vision is shared by no one is a dreamer; the person whose vision is supported by the organization is a leader.

CONCLUSION

My question is simple: Do you want to be a leader? Someone has invested her confidence and resources in you; that is why you are in your current professional position. Someone saw leadership qualities in you and appointed you a manager. Your challenge is to take full advantage of the opportunity you have been given and to become a distinguished leader of those within your current *and future* spheres of influence.

- *Practice discipline:* Do what is necessary, not what is easy.
- *Remain humble:* Remember the influence you have, and cherish it as a precious commodity.
- *Always be accountable* for your actions.

- *Persevere:* If something were easy to do, it likely would already have been done.
- *Be a person of vision:* Don't be afraid to challenge the current system and to set higher expectations.

20

CHAPTER TWENTY

Lessons Learned

JANET WARD

When I

entered the profession in 1978, the phrase "enrollment management" was non-existent. One worked for admissions, financial aid, student accounts, or registration and records, and each department worked independently from the others. Most professionals specialized in one area (*e.g.*, admissions) and then spent their entire career in that field. My own career has traversed the enrollment spectrum; along the way, I've picked up several kernels of wisdom.

LESSON ONE: BUILD YOUR BRAND

Whether you are starting your first professional position, moving up the career ladder, or entering a new institution, it is important that you control your brand. For what do you want to be remembered? How will you choose to work with your staff and colleagues? As you work through challenges, disappointments, and crises, your words and actions will be remembered and judged by others. You have a choice, either to "take control of your brand" by taking responsibility for your words and actions or allowing others to create it for you.

Become a lifelong learner: Change is inevitable. Successful enrollment professionals have an innate desire to continually learn new techniques, processes, tools and become skilled at adapting to change. Learning is tied to achieving your institution's business objectives. This can be accomplished by streamlining a process to reduce overhead, re-aligning staff assignments to maximize productivity, or enhancing the experience of higher education consumers (*e.g.*, prospect, admit, enrolled student, alumnus, parent, donor).

Character matters: Honesty, ethics, sound decision-making, and how you treat others combine to tell your story. Your words, actions and principles must consistently transcend any situation. You are the same in any situation, regardless of the pressure you are under. This requires developing the ability to work effectively in various situations with various personalities while managing differing points of view.

LESSON TWO: BECOME AN ASTUTE OBSERVER

I started my career as a manager of off-site community college programs. Asked if I wanted a typewriter on my desk (my boss had one on his), I told him that I would rely on the support staff for this function; after all, I had noticed that the other program managers (all men) relied on the administrative assistants when they needed to have something typed. I believe as a result of my choice, my male colleagues more readily accepted me as a partner and an equal in the operation of the department. I believe that if I had placed a typewriter on my desk, I would have been perceived—and treated—as a member of the secretarial pool. And while the secretarial pool's members were all wonderful women, I wanted to be treated as a manager.

"Walk the floor" to understand your business and people. Listen. One of the greatest lessons I learned early in my career was the value of taking the time to rotate through every position within the department. Not only did I learn each function firsthand, I also learned about and from each staff member—challenges, what did not work, ideas to improve operations. As a result, the staff and I grew to trust one another and to work together to implement needed changes. For example, a staff member who was instrumental in marketing a specialized program needed to improve her public speaking skills. How did I motivate her? I challenged her, by telling her to face her fear by taking a public speaking class, and I in turn would confront one of my fears. I felt proud when she received top honors in her course and even more so as she became a more effective admissions counselor.

LESSON THREE: LEAD BY EXAMPLE

Expectations are part of the job: set clear performance expectations, and hold staff accountable from the outset. I put my performance expectations in writing and then refine them after seeking staff input. Once finalized, the expectations become part of the annual review process; staff members are held accountable. Remember that your staff will expect you to meet any expectation you set for them. If you want your staff to be punctual, then you must be punctual. If you want your management team to effectively address personnel issues, you need to demonstrate these skills and teach them to your team and serve as their mentor.

Choose to act rather than react: Others will observe how you handle difficult situations, and many will emulate your behavior. My personal philosophy is that much of life is out of my control: organizations change, technology changes, and staff come and go. The only area I know I can control is how I choose to act or what I choose to say. When confronted with a demanding situation, I compose my facial expression so as not to give away what I am thinking while I consider the alternatives. Once I have made my choice, I carefully phrase my response. Words are powerful, so choose wisely such that your viewpoint will have the best chance of being heard. Many arguments could be avoided if we simply imagine ourselves in the other's position, consider his thoughts and feelings, and then respond in a way that takes his needs into account.

Be transparent: be kind, and be firm. Working with people can be one of the most exhausting jobs. As the size of your staff increases, so will the the variety of personalities you encournter. You need to become both an effective manager (about the task) and supervisor (about the people). Most staff members appreciate a boss who is consistent, transparent, kind, and firm. Being transparent means not having hidden agendas or "playing favorites" in the office. Keep your staff informed about what is happening on campus. The only information I don't routinely share with my staff pertains to personnel matters.

Be kind. Life is a journey, and each of us, at different times, will benefit from a kind word, encouragement, or forgiveness. As the saying goes, "what goes around comes around." If you want to be treated with kindness, then be considerate of others.

Be firm—the counterpoint to compassion. The challenge for any leader is to find the right balance between the two. We all make mistakes. A good leader encourages staff to step forward and acknowledge what failed so that training may occur to ultimately improve services, programs, operations. If training has occurred and errors continue, then be firm and handle the situation appropriately; this may require you to dismiss the employee (though I believe everyone deserves a second chance). Too many times, I've seen poor performance excused; the result has been that the entire department—and/or "downstream" processes—pay the price for on-going ineptitude. Be firm when you need to be. After all, leaders have to make tough decisions.

LESSON FOUR: THE ART OF GETTING THINGS DONE

Learn the political landscape. To be effective within your department or college, you need to understand organizational politics—

"the art of getting things done." In a healthy organization, true leaders are able to find common ground (despite diverse points of view on a variety of topics) and focus on furthering the institution's mission. Leaders remain open to exploring new ideas; operate transparently and hold few institutional secrets; and base decisions on sound principles and good data.

Movers and shakers propel our institutions forward. These individuals are able to influence others, build an action plan, and then implement the plan so as to achieve the desired business objective. Movers and shakers may include frontline staff, managers or executives; it is more about the person than the position. Movers and shakers should be highly prized as they know how to get things done.

Manage your time well: Time is a precious commodity that, once lost, cannot be recaptured. If it is managed effectively, significant progress can be made toward achieving goals. Effective time management starts with your calendar. Review the past few months and consider how your time was spent. Then consider the following questions:

- Did you allocate time to such value-added activities as planning, assessment, staff development, and your own professional development?
- Did your meetings result in tangible outcomes or action plans that moved the organization forward in achieving its business objectives?
- Did you control your calendar by scheduling uninterrupted work time at your desk (*e.g.*, no phone calls, no e-mail, etc.)?
- Is your staff cross-trained so that every critical business process has a back-up—that is, if one person is absent, can operations continue unimpeded?
- When you leave work at the end of the day or for vacation, do you "disconnect" (*i.e.*, leave work at work)?

If you answered yes to all five questions, then congratulations: you've demonstrated that you are the boss of your time. If you answered no to any of the questions, then you have some work to do to improve your time management skills. Here are some techniques I've found effective in managing my time and multiple projects:

- Create a master task list with start and end dates that includes recurring projects for you and your staff. Review the list every Monday, marking off those that have been completed and following up on any that are past due.
- Before leaving work on Friday, review your own task list and prioritize what you'll focus on in the coming week.
- Each week, inform your staff that a specific day/time on your calendar has been blocked off for planning. Unless a crisis requires immediate action, do not accept phone calls or check e-mail during this time.
- Whenever you facilitate a meeting, be sure to provide an agenda in advance that is focused on achieving specific business objective(s). After the meeting, send out minutes that highlight the key discussion points and action steps as well as who is responsible for each. If you are invited to meetings that do not adhere to this format, encourage the facilitator to adopt it—and/or consider opting out of the meeting in the future.
- Schedule a planning day each month when you work from home, uninterrupted. This can be a great opportunity to catch up on reading.
- Consider closing the office at specific times during the year for staff development that is focused on improving operations and the student experience, or learning new technology.

LESSON FIVE: ENJOY LIFE'S JOURNEY

I learned one of my greatest life lessons from my father: Life is short, so live each day with zest and energy. At points in my career and life when I have felt under-valued, I have learned to close that chapter and move on. Know when it is time to dust off the resume, and have the courage to act. You never will know what you are capable of unless you try.

Balance work and play. Some of my colleagues are amazed when I go on vacation and disconnect completely from work—no e-mails, no phone calls. I am able to do this for two reasons: I have built my leadership team so they can handle any situation; they know I trust their judgment. The second reason is self-discipline: I choose to disconnect by not checking my e-mail. With the benefit of rest and a change of pace, I return to work re-energized and ready to invest myself fully in the work of the university.

Leave work at work. When at work, give your best effort; when you leave at the end of the day, turn work off. Do not check your e-mail. Do not take work home with you (you may have to make rare exceptions). Invest in yourself. Learn a new hobby; find something you are passionate about and pursue it. Take time to exercise, eat nutritionally, and get a good night's rest.

Finally, laugh more, and celebrate the simple joys. In the blink of an eye, you will be approaching retirement and, I hope, looking back over a career filled with accomplishments, joy, and friendships.

21

CHAPTER TWENTY-ONE

On Leadership

BETH L. WECKMUELLER

The invitation

to share some thoughts about leadership and mentorship in our profession came at an interesting time. There has been a major reorganization at my university, and I've just recently stepped aside from my familiar role as head of our enrollment services unit, handing over the reins of "my" department—as I have thought of it for almost two decades—to others. In my new role, I am involved primarily in research, planning, and policy development, interesting work that I very much enjoy. But while I still consult and advise the new management team, it is clearly now their operation to lead, not mine. So perhaps this is indeed the perfect time to reflect. How did I get here, and what did I learn along the way that might be helpful for our new leaders to know?

My own path to what has been an immensely gratifying career in enrollment management was unplanned and really quite serendipitous: I was your typical (in the 1970s, anyway) left-leaning wannabe intellectual and started my career in higher education teaching German. I had also worked as an editor, copywriter, and translator (not to mention some formative early years in the food service industry). When I attended graduate school, degree programs with names like "college student personnel" did not exist (or, if they did, I was completely unaware of them). And, like many colleagues of my generation, I doubt I had ever heard the term "enrollment management" when I first was hired into an administrative position in what was then (as again now) simply called the registrar's office.

But that first job—a summer gig deciphering fairly technical systems documentation and trying to render it into reader-friendly training materials—soon turned into another, and another, until before I knew it I was a newly minted, still very wet-behind-the-ears assistant director with a dozen or so much older and wiser staff reporting to me. No, those seasoned civil servants were not particularly thrilled with their newbie boss—and quite rightly so. I did work very hard; I found a mentor; I gradually figured out how much I did not know and how to set about learning all that I needed to know; and eventually, things turned out all right. But when I think of how fundamentally unqualified I was for that first leadership role and of how many mistakes I made in those early years, I still blush with embarrassment.

Perhaps it is because I came into that first management position so woefully ill-prepared that I have tried to be especially patient with and helpful to staff who are at that early stage in their careers. Our first-time supervisors and managers do make mistakes; often don't know what all they don't know; and sometimes have overly high opinions of themselves. "Hold the drama and just get a grip!" we oldsters are tempted to advise, muttering to ourselves about the younger generation. But really, who among us has not been there and done—or failed to do—that?

In recent years, I also tried to be intentional about succession planning for my department. I worked to develop new talent and to anticipate how best to prepare our emerging leaders to climb the next rung on the organizational ladder. And now these plans seem to be coming to fruition, whether or not we are all quite ready. Several on our new leadership team are staff I hired, worked with for many years, and consider friends as well as colleagues. Far from being newbies, they are mostly quite experienced, and all are tremendously competent. While I certainly tried my best to coach and mentor them over the years, help them advance their careers, and prepare for a leadership transition such as this, most of the credit goes to them for their own initiative and hard work. They are ready, and I believe they will do very well. But of course I can't help but wonder: Did I do all I could to help them prepare for this next step? And what, specifically, did I hope to impart with regard to leadership skills?

I can't really answer that first question. Because this transition is still so new, it's too soon to know how well I did to help them prepare. And anyway, you'd have to ask them. You might even have to check back in a year or two. But I have been contemplating the second question; and although I never made a list of all I hoped to impart with regard to leadership, certain themes and characteristics stand out and have come up often in conversations with younger colleagues.

The attributes of leadership that I find most important reflect lessons I've learned both from my own mentors and role models and from (sometimes painful!) personal experience. Of course, there are many other skills and abilities that are no less critical for successful leaders in our profession, ranging from familiarity with new technology to adaptability to change, from negotiation and coalition-building to effective communication—all resting on a strong and deep foundation of subject matter expertise. But as it happens, the traits I prefer to focus on are not specific to leadership within enrollment management, or even higher education administration. That may be due to the motley crew who comprise my own set of most valued mentors/models, since in addition to a few university administrators, they include at least one chef (a hard-working, open minded, iconoclastic breed to whom I think we should pay closer attention); a very proper, conservative, old-school lawyer; and several pointy-headed academic types who were not in fact very good at administration but who taught me a thing or two about intellectual rigor and the persuasive power of a well-reasoned argument. Go figure: I guess it's true that our best teachers find us, rather than vice versa.

So here are a few of my thoughts about what it takes to be an effective leader today—not only in our profession but, I would wager, in many others as well:

FIND YOUR OWN STYLE, FASHIONABLE OR NOT.

Perhaps I should preface this by saying that I'm not a huge fan of many of the characteristics-of-leadership guides one finds today on the how-to shelves at the bookstore. Too many, it seems to me, prescribe a one-size-fits-all approach that in fact is ill-suited to many personality types. All this talk about being bold, forceful, and charismatic threatens to leave more than half of the population feeling that they may not have what it takes. Don't get me wrong: If you are a natural extrovert who finds it easy to show your passion and give motivational speeches, then by all means harness your energy, emotion, and high spirits to rev up your team. Inspirational pep talks and high fives all around for jobs well done may be your forte, and if so, good for you! But what if you are the quieter, more cerebral type, still passionate but maybe not so gregarious, not so good at the rah-rah? What if you need to quietly think things through before responding rather than being the first one out of the gate? On my list, that's okay, too. Trust yourself, and you ultimately will find that there are many ways to lead effectively. No, you can't just hide out in your office; you do have to connect with people and communicate. But don't worry: the low-key approach can work just fine. Bold ideas may be expressed quietly as well as loudly.

Remain calm, and carry on. Whatever their personal style, the best leaders remain calm and collected, no matter what. They never panic, especially when something goes really wrong (or threatens to). Like the most skilled chess (or tennis) players, they are very good at thinking several moves (or strokes) ahead, anticipating consequences, pro or con, that others might overlook in the heat of the moment. Calm in this context does not mean complacent or disinterested, though it does mean not yelling and not blaming. A calm and centered leader will find that people are far more likely to admit mistakes and problems, to tell the truth and seek help in finding a solution, than to cover up the mess. A calm leader doesn't make a bad situation worse by overreacting or by letting disappointment or anger get in the way of an effective solution. She thinks the problem through, helps determine the best way to address it, and then takes corrective action as needed to deal with the cause. Calmly.

TRY TO SAY YES—BUT DON'T BE AFRAID TO SAY NO.

I've often remarked that I built a successful career by saying yes. Yes to challenging assignments and new responsibilities, often uncompensated. Yes to sometimes ridiculous deadlines, yes to bosses and colleagues and staff, yes to countless "Can we somehow make this work?" requests, some of them awfully inconvenient. Saying yes is powerful and can help you empower others. It shows confidence and can make you an especially valued employee or colleague. But yes is not *always* the right answer, and the best leaders know when the answer needs to be no. Perhaps it's an ethical issue—someone leaning on you to cross a line you know should not be crossed. Perhaps it's a spectacularly ill-conceived new initiative that you know will harm your operation and demoralize your staff. Whatever the case, when that happens, a strong and effective leader will figure out how to say no, even if that involves some personal risk—because in fact leaders who say no may not always get their way.

Sometimes they are overruled, and when that happens they will have to decide how to respond. But so be it. They will be respected, and they will sleep well at night.

LOVE YOUR PEOPLE LIKE FAMILY. REALLY.

Some version of this appears on most traits-of-leadership lists, so I claim no originality, except to emphasize the "like family" part. Of course, all aspiring leaders will say that it takes a village...that they are nothing without the staff who support them...that they are fortunate to have a fabulous and beloved team...etc. But how do the most effective leaders really act? To truly love your people—and here I mean especially the people whose boss you are—*like family* entails certain obligations. It means, for instance, that you don't speak ill of your people to others; nor do you casually let others do so. Nobody gets to bash your people, period. When one of them screws up—and they will (heck, even if you don't *like* him very much at the moment)—you listen, do what you can to help fix the problem, and get things back on track. You may need to have a heart-to-heart conversation or take other corrective action later, of course. But ultimately, you try to be kind, forgive him or her, and move on, just as you do with your own family, no matter how annoyed you sometimes may be.

REMEMBER THAT IT IS NOT ALL ABOUT YOU.

Finally, if there is one thing I most hope to have successfully modeled for the emerging leaders with whom I have worked over the years, this might be it. The best leaders, in my opinion, are self-confident but not full of themselves. They are serious about their work and the success of their organization—in our profession, they are serious about promoting and supporting our students, faculty, and staff in the complicated but noble enterprise that is higher education—but they are, ultimately, humble. The most effective leaders keep the big picture in mind, understand they are part of a much greater whole, and are able to interpret and convey this larger context to their staff in ways they all can embrace. The most effective leaders admit their mistakes and are not afraid to laugh at themselves. Even in adversity, they choose the high road. And of course, true leaders understand that when something goes well in their sphere of influence, the best thing to do is to give their people the credit, taking little or none for themselves. This is not only generous but wise as these leaders have learned that, like love, the more credit you give away, the more will come back to you.

22

CHAPTER TWENTY-TWO

Leadership Lessons for New Professionals

LOUISE LONABOCKER

Forty years

ago, I arrived in Boston with an associate's degree and two years' experience in the corporate world. The idea of working at a college appealed, so I boarded the B line trolley to Boston College. I arrived on campus, found the human resources office, took a typing test, interviewed with the director of freshman financial aid, and received an offer of employment the following week. I've been there ever since.

Over the years, I admittedly have been in the right place at the right time. My career trajectory was fast, as was often the case in those days. After serving for three years in two support positions, I was given responsibility for transfer admission. Three years later, I moved to the registrar's office, where I served as assistant and then associate registrar; I was promoted to registrar by the time I was 30 years old. Simultaneously, I continued my undergraduate and graduate education; in 1981, I earned a Ph.D. in higher education administration from Boston College.

Not only was I in the right place at the right time, but I also had the privilege of working with leaders and mentors who went on to become nationally recognized experts in enrollment management, information technology, and testing and measurement. These leaders taught me countless lessons, some of which I share here.

HIRE THE BEST

Great leaders surround themselves with outstanding people. As one graduate school instructor admonished, "Never be afraid to hire good people, they'll always make you look good." Exemplary leaders assign responsibility, hold employees accountable, offer advice and support, stay out of the way, allow employees to learn from their mistakes by helping with the recovery, and celebrate accomplishments. Leaders advocate for staff, support their development, capitalize on their strengths, and encourage them to take on new challenges. Leaders find creative ways to retain the best employees; these may include flexible work schedules, telecommuting, and short leaves to accommodate unexpected life events. Leaders know it's the little things that mean a lot—for example, casual Fridays, lunch or snacks during peak times of busyness, and recognition for work well done. We are fortunate to also have the opportunity to train and develop student employees and graduate assistants, who bring skills, talent, energy, and insight to the organization. Encourage everyone to contribute, listen to their ideas, and serve them well. In turn, they will serve you—and your institution—well.

EMBRACE CHANGE

Early in my career, paper was everywhere. But as computers arrived, automation began both at the institutional level and on the desktop. One mentor, always on the prowl for the next technological "edge," taught me the value of projects that resulted in broad, sweeping change. In those days, that meant distributing transactions to end users that included academic departments, students, and faculty. Today, similar transformations are being wrought by social media, digital documents, data marts, open source, cloud computing, and mobile applications. Many trends begin outside higher education; the smart leader follows and learns from these. (Banking, retail, travel, and other industries often are among the early adopters of new technologies and services—for example, online chat.) Be alert to customer services that please you—the bottle of water offered by a car rental agency during check-in or an impressive service recovery after a transaction gone bad. Learn from these interactions, and evaluate the potential for developing similar practices on your campus.

KEEP LOOKING FOR WAYS TO IMPROVE

Most of us do not have the opportunity to be involved in transformational change on an ongoing basis. But continuous improvement is something to which we should aspire all the time. Each year, I prepare goals for the office for the upcoming year, link them to university strategic goals (where applicable), and share them with staff. Staff members incorporate the goals into their annual reports, in which they are encouraged to describe their own accomplishments and goals; these subsequently inform performance appraisals. A chart of noteworthy accomplishments from the past decade hangs in one of our common areas to remind staff that we are always on the quest to improve processes. Improvements include small projects like creating a Facebook presence, technical projects like issuing electronic refunds, and major projects like implementing a curriculum management system. Improvements may be identified as a result of inviting staff to tinker with an iPad or Google Apps to search for potential applications for these technologies; asking for ideas for improvement after major events like the opening of school; or taking staff to a local deli that demonstrates outstanding teamwork and customer service. The key is to foster an environment that encourages staff to value teamwork, to offer their ideas for operating more efficiently and effectively, and to foster mechanisms by which to provide the best possible customer service.

IT'S ALL ABOUT THE DATA

One mentor was a firm believer in metrics and measures. Data proved the facts and were used to drive decision making. I learned that you can talk and provide anecdotal information all you want, but nothing is as persuasive as data to prove trends or identify patterns, as in enrollment, retention, advanced placement, telephone usage, appeals, etc. If you support your requests with data that you understand, you will increase the likelihood of achieving desired outcomes.

GET INVOLVED

At the start of my career, I worked and attended classes and did not devote a lot of time to professional activities. That changed in 1981, when I joined my first AACRAO committee. There I met an extraordinary group of local professionals and national leaders who were always willing to share their knowledge. I discovered that by becoming more engaged, I could get to know people who had developed expertise in a wide range of areas, from compliance to technology to leadership. Joining committees and task forces not only brought me into contact with leaders in the profession but also deepened my knowledge by requiring me to prepare presentations, write articles, and research institutional practices. Now, when an issue arises, I know how to research the subject, identify experts, and contact them for further information, as needed. The same holds true for institutional engagement, to include volunteering for committee membership and professional development opportunities. These types of involvement brought me into contact with a wide range of people and practices across campus—athletics, financial services, accreditation, study abroad, and performance management. Such wide-ranging involvement positioned me to lead Boston College's one-stop student services organization when it was formed almost fifteen years ago.

READ

Another way to engage with the profession is to read periodicals, journals, books, and publications. This is a perfect way to supplement or even supplant conference attendance and to stay abreast of professional standards and practices, regulatory compliance, new technologies, and trends in higher education. I read AACRAO publications to keep current with professional standards and practices, *The Chronicle of Higher Education* for depth and breadth of awareness of higher education issues, *Educause Review* for new technologies and applications, and the education and business sections of *The New York Times* for breaking news. Certainly, there are many other worthy publications, and you can choose your favorites. You also can participate in webinars, read blogs, and follow the Twitter accounts of your favorite professionals. The important thing is to devote up to 20 percent of your time to lifelong learning.

TALK, WRITE, LISTEN

I am not by nature an extrovert, but neither do I find it difficult to start a conversation with a conference participant by asking what's new on her campus, commenting on a presentation she delivered, or asking about her involvement in the association. Such discussions may include mention of an idea you can implement on your campus or may lead to collaboration on a presentation or a site visit to another campus. If you are not in a position to attend conferences, then take part in similar discussions by joining listservs (or by creating your own!). I get answers to questions quickly by emailing the registrars at Jesuit institutions, Boston universities, and Atlantic Coast Conference (ACC) schools.

EXPLORE THE WORLD OF HIGHER EDUCATION

I love to travel, and I enjoy visiting other campuses. As I'm able, I invite colleagues to lunch to talk about developments on their campuses. Sometimes I join an admissions tour or just walk around on my own and observe signage, publications, classrooms, office layouts, and hospitality. It's a good way to take a fresh look at how institutions present themselves and to return with ideas that can be introduced on your own campus.

COMMUNICATE YOUR MESSAGE

Communication is a challenging process of balancing exchanges in meetings, conference calls, video conferences, and webinars with the uninterrupted time staff need to fulfill their roles and responsibilities. Fortunately, many modes of communication reduce the need for in-person meetings and facilitate information sharing (consider, for example, email, newsletters, and blogs). In addition to weekly meetings with senior staff, committee meetings, and project meetings, I enjoy getting together with the entire staff once or twice a year to review recent office accomplishments, reiterate goals for the upcoming year, and highlight institutional goals. Initiate communication with external audiences to help ensure that students do not miss important dates and deadlines related to financial aid, graduation, course withdrawals and drops, and account resolution. New students benefit from welcome checklists, guidance about student employment, and online and print FAQs. Proactive and "just-in-time" communication will minimize reactive customer outbursts and complaints.

DON'T FORGET TO RELAX

I noted early that my mentors led balanced lives, and I have attempted to do the same. I am focused at work, and when I leave work, I shift my focus to family, friends, reading, exercise, travel, cultural activities, volunteer work, or spirituality. After a stressful week at work, treat yourself to a massage, sports event, movie, museum, or other relaxing and stress-relieving activity. Observing and enjoying life and letting your mind wander are often the best ways to gain insight into a problem or to experience an "a-ha" moment.

Even after 40 years, I still look forward to coming to work in the morning, to seeing the construction on a new humanities building, to anticipating the university's 150th anniversary, to following emerging trends in higher education, to marveling at new technologies, and to listening to the good ideas of my colleagues. And to think that this satisfying and rewarding career started with a convenient ride on the T!

References & Recommended Reading

REFERENCES

Bennis, W.G. 1989. *On Becoming a Leader*. New York: Basic Books.

———. 1994. *On Becoming a Leader*. Cambridge, MA: Perseus Books.

Blanchard, K., S.M. Bowles, D. Carew, and E. Parisi-Carew. 2000. *High Five: The Magic of Working Together*. New York: William Morrow.

Covey, S.R. 2002. Foreword. In *Servant Leadership: A Journey into the Nature of Legitimate Power and Greatness / Essays by Robert K. Greenleaf*, edited by L.C. Spears. Mahwah, NJ: Paulist Press.

Cramer, S.F. 2005. *Student Information Systems: A Guide to Implementation Success*. Washington, DC: American Association of Collegiate Registrars and Admissions Officers.

Gardner, J.W. 1961. *Excellence: Can We Be Equal and Excellent Too?* New York: Harper and Row.

———. 1990. *On Leadership*. New York: The Free Press.

Haab, M., and S.F. Cramer. 2011. Enterprise resource planning systems in higher education. In *Technology Integration in Higher Education: Social and Organizational Aspects*, edited by D.W. Surry, J. Stefurak, and R. Gray. Hershey, PA: IGI Global.

Hossler, D., and J. Bean. 1990. *The Strategic Management of College Enrollments*. San Francisco: Jossey Bass.

Kaplan, R.S., and D.P. Norton. 2004. Keeping score on community investment. *Leader to Leader*. 33: 13–19.

Kelley, S. 2012, August 2. Mariners are better off without Ichiro. Seattle Times. Available at: <http://seattletimes.com/html/stevekelley/2018836471_kelley03.html>.

Kouzes, J.M., and B.Z. Posner. 1990. *The Leadership Challenge: How to Get Extraordinary Things Done in Organizations*. San Francisco: Jossey Bass.

Mohr, N., and A. Dichter. 2001. Building a learning organization. *Phi Delta Kappan*. 82(10): 744–747.

Rath, T., and B. Conchie. 2008. *Strengths Based Leadership*. New York: Gallup Press.

RECOMMENDED READING

Covey, S.R. 2004. *The Seven Habits of Highly Effective People.* New York: Simon and Schuster.

De Pree, M. 1989. *Leadership Is an Art.* New York: Doubleday.

———. 1992. *Leadership Jazz.* New York: Doubleday.

Gardner, J.W. 1990. *On Leadership.* New York: The Free Press.

Greenleaf, R.K. 1977. *Servant Leadership: A Journey into the Nature of Legitimate Power and Greatness.* Mahwah, NJ: Paulist Press.

Kouzes, J.M., B.Z. Posner. 2007. *The Leadership Challenge,* 5th ed. San Francisco: Jossey Bass.